D1372322

DOODLE
LIT

FOR SAM, OLIVIA,
HENRY, AND HAZEL
—J.A.

◆◆

FOR NINA & SCOTT
—A.O.

DOODLE LIT

By

JENNIFER ADAMS _____ **ALISON OLIVER**

YOUR NAME

TEXT © 2014 JENNIFER ADAMS
ILLUSTRATIONS © 2014 ALISON OLIVER

DESIGNED BY ALISON OLIVER
MANUFACTURED IN HONG KONG IN
JUNE 2014 BY PARAMOUNT PRINTING CO., LTD.

GIBBS SMITH BOOKS ARE PRINTED ON PAPER PRODUCED FROM
SUSTAINABLE PEFC-CERTIFIED FOREST/CONTROLLED WOOD SOURCE.
LEARN MORE AT WWW.PEFC.ORG.

PUBLISHED BY
GIBBS SMITH
P.O. BOX 667
LAYTON, UTAH 84041

1.800.835.4993 ORDERS
WWW.GIBBS-SMITH.COM

ISBN: 978-1-4236-3551-2

FIRST EDITION
18 17 16 15 14   5 4 3 2 1

INTRODUCTION

JENNIFER ON DOODLING

DOODLING IS SUCH A SIMPLE FORM OF BEING CREATIVE. WHEN YOU DOODLE, YOU USUALLY ALLOW YOURSELF TO DO IT FREELY—YOU'RE NOT TRYING TO MAKE A FINAL PIECE OF ART OR WORRYING WHAT SOMEONE ELSE WILL THINK. IT'S JUST A SIMPLE, CREATIVE EXPRESSION. I DOODLE WHEN I'M ON THE PHONE, WHEN I'M BORED, OR WHEN I'M STUCK ON A WRITING OR EDITING PROBLEM THAT TAKES TIME TO FIX.

THIS JOURNAL IS FILLED WITH PROMPTS TO GET YOU STARTED DOODLING AND TO GENERATE IDEAS. AND THEY'RE ALL BASED ON THE CLASSICS. WE LOVE THE RATS IN *DRACULA*, THE BUGGIES IN *PRIDE AND PREJUDICE*, AND ALL THE ANIMALS IN *THE JUNGLE BOOK*. *DOODLELIT* GIVES YOU PROMPTS FOR ALMOST EVERYTHING UNDER THE SUN!

DOODLE FOR FUN! BE CREATIVE AND EXPLORE IDEAS. IT WOULD BE A GOOD IDEA TO TRY DIFFERENT PENCILS, PAINTS, MARKERS, CRAYONS, AND INK ON DIFFERENT PAGES IN THIS BOOK. FEEL FREE TO TEAR PAGES OUT OR ADD YOUR OWN PAGES IN. CUT THINGS FROM MAGAZINES OR ADD PHOTOS IF YOU LIKE. EMBELLISH YOUR DOODLES WITH GLITTER, RIBBON,

BUTTONS, THREAD, OR SEQUINS, OR WITH LITTLE PIECES OF
THINGS YOU FIND IN NATURE, LIKE GRASSES OR FEATHERS
OR LEAVES.

WHEN YOU'RE YOUNG, YOU'RE SMART ENOUGH TO KNOW
THAT ART IS FUN. WHEN WE GET OLDER, SOMETIMES WE
FORGET THAT. ART IS FUN! JUST DOODLE. :D

ᵠᵠᵠᵠᵠᵠᵠᵠᵠᵠᵠᵠᵠᵠᵠᵠᵠᵠᵠᵠᵠᵠᵠᵠᵠᵠᵠᵠᵠᵠᵠᵠᵠᵠᵠ

ALISON ON DOODLING

THERE IS MAGIC IN DOODLING. WHEN YOU DRAW OR DOODLE
WITHOUT PLANNING AND THINKING YOU LET YOUR CREATIVITY
REVEAL ITSELF WITHOUT YOUR BRAIN GETTING IN THE WAY,
SO WHATEVER YOU MAKE HAS A STORY TO TELL YOU.

DOODLING CAN MAKE YOU FEEL CALM AND RELAXED, IT CAN
HELP YOU WHEN YOU WANT TO COME UP WITH AN IDEA FOR
A PROJECT, OR IT CAN JUST BE FOR FUN. WHEN I WANT TO
START AN ILLUSTRATION I ALWAYS DOODLE FIRST. SOMETIMES
I DRAW A VERY SMALL PART OF THE SUBJECT OVER AND OVER
TO SEE WHAT WILL HAPPEN. OFTEN IT TAKES ME TO A PLACE
I WASN'T EXPECTING. OTHER TIMES I DRAW SOMETHING OVER
AND OVER AND I LOOK BACK AT THE FIRST ONE AND REALIZE

THE ESSENCE OF WHAT I WANTED IS RIGHT THERE IN THAT
FIRST MESSY DOODLE—NO MATTER WHAT IT LOOKS LIKE
TO SOMEBODY ELSE. THE INFORMATION IN THERE IS JUST
WHAT I NEED TO GO TO THE NEXT STEP.

DOODLING REALLY SAVES THE DAY FOR ME WHEN MY BRAIN
CAN'T SEEM TO FIND A SOLUTION TO A CHALLENGE OR COME
UP WITH AN INTERESTING APPROACH TO A DRAWING; I
START WITH SOMETHING—ANYTHING!—A LINE OR A SYMBOL,
SOMETIMES A WORD THAT MAKES ME THINK OF ANOTHER
WORD OR PROMPTS ME TO DRAW WHAT THAT WORD SOUNDS
LIKE. BEFORE LONG I HAVE SOMETHING ON PAPER THAT IS
SHOWING ME THE ANSWER LIKE A MAP LEADING ME TO A
TREASURE. FOR THAT REASON ALONE I WOULD SUGGEST THAT
ALL DOODLES ARE PERFECT DOODLES!

IN THESE PAGES YOU WILL FIND SOME SAMPLES OF DOODLES
BY VERY FAMOUS WRITERS. WE FOUND THESE DOODLES IN
THEIR JOURNALS AND THE MARGINS OF THEIR MANUSCRIPTS.
IT IS FUN TO SEE HOW THEIR DRAWINGS RELATE TO WHAT
THEY WERE WRITING ABOUT AT THE TIME. AND WE HAVE
LEFT SPACE FOR YOU TO DOODLE AROUND THEM AND IMAGINE
WHAT YOU MIGHT DOODLE IF YOU WERE THAT PERSON.
FILL THESE PAGES WITH WHAT THEIR DOODLES INSPIRE YOU
TO EXPLORE.

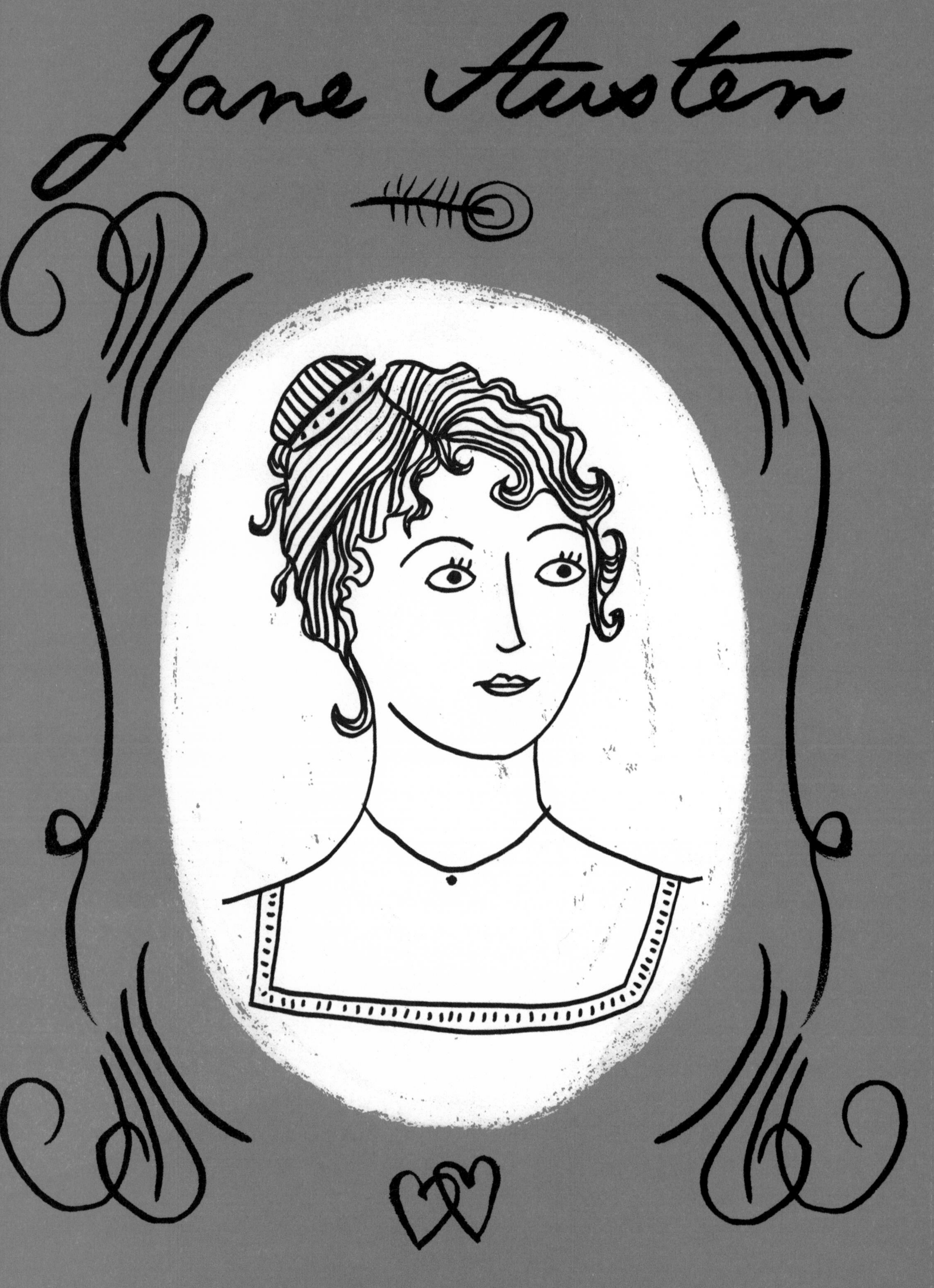
Jane Austen

"A LADY'S IMAGINATION IS VERY RAPID; IT JUMPS FROM ADMIRATION TO LOVE, FROM LOVE TO DOODLING..."
—JANE AUSTEN

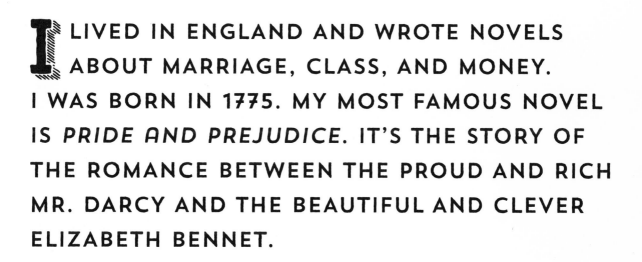

I LIVED IN ENGLAND AND WROTE NOVELS ABOUT MARRIAGE, CLASS, AND MONEY. I WAS BORN IN 1775. MY MOST FAMOUS NOVEL IS *PRIDE AND PREJUDICE*. IT'S THE STORY OF THE ROMANCE BETWEEN THE PROUD AND RICH MR. DARCY AND THE BEAUTIFUL AND CLEVER ELIZABETH BENNET.

AND DON'T FORGET
MY SOCKS—I LIKE
FANCY SOCKS!

WHAT KIND OF DOG DOES MR. DARCY HAVE?
DOODLE IT AND GIVE IT A NAME.

ADD NAME
TO BOWL

LONGBOURN

NETHERFIELD

THIS IS A
TOPIARY

PEMBERLEY

DRAW YOUR OWN HOUSE.

(AND ADD SOME CUSTOM TOPIARIES!*)

* A TOPIARY IS A TREE OR BUSH THAT HAS BEEN TRIMMED TO GROW IN A CERTAIN SHAPE. SOME TOPIARIES LOOK LIKE BALLS OR CONES. SOME LOOK LIKE ANIMALS!

BALL GOWNS

COLOR THESE AND CUT THEM OUT
TO MAKE AN ELIZABETH BENNET
PAPER DOLL AND HER CLOTHING.

YOU CAN DESIGN YOUR OWN
DRESSES FOR HER, TOO!

PETTICOATS:

A PETTICOAT IS A SLIP OF FABRIC WORN
UNDER A DRESS. STIFF PETTICOATS
WITH RUFFLES CAN MAKE A SKIRT PUFF
OUT MORE.

MAKE THE GLOVES
MATCH HER DRESS...
OR NOT!

GIVE LIZZIE A PRETTY
NECKLACE TO WEAR

PUT A FLOWER IN
LIZZIE'S HAIR

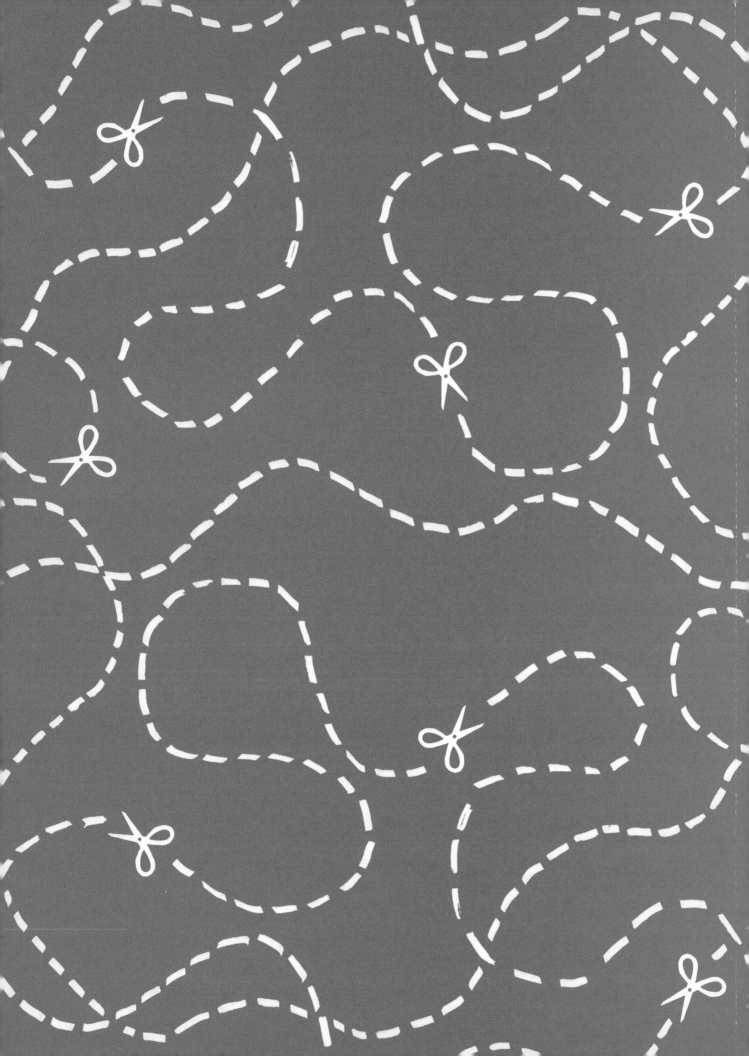

DOODLE DESIGNS ON THESE HEARTS.

FOLLOW THE STEPS TO DRAW YOUR OWN SHEEP.

1

LEAVE THE FACE EMPTY SO YOU CAN DRAW AN EYE

2

NOW FILL IT IN

3

ADD LEGS

4

FILL THE FIELD WITH SHEEP!

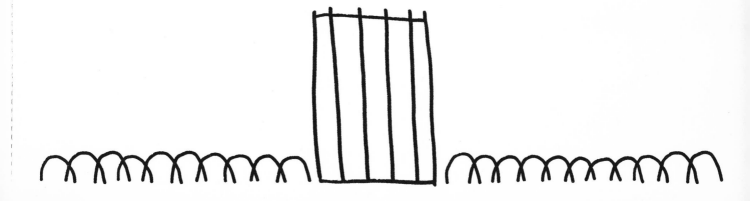

BFFs

ELIZABETH BENNET LIKES TO HANG
OUT WITH HER SISTERS. DRAW PICTURES
OF YOU AND YOUR FRIENDS.

ADD SOME
DETAIL TO
THESE FRAMES

HOT ROD BUGGIES!

CUSTOMIZE THESE BUGGIES FOR THE BENNETS.

USE PATTERNS, COLORS,
STICKERS, GLITTER, AND WHATEVER
ELSE YOU CAN FIND.

LET'S PLAY!

THIS GUY PLAYS THE CELLO.
WHAT INSTRUMENT DO YOU WANT TO PLAY?
DOODLE THE INSTRUMENTS ON THE NEXT PAGE.

FLUTE

FRENCH HORN

DRUMS

VIOLIN

TRUMPET

HAVE A BALL!

❖

ELIZABETH AND MR. DARCY MET AT A BALL.
DRAW PEOPLE DANCING IN
THEIR FANCY PARTY CLOTHES.

MAKING MONEY

THE BRITISH POUND:
THE BRITISH POUND IS THE OFFICIAL MONEY OF ENGLAND. THE FULL, OFFICIAL NAME IS "POUND STERLING."

DESIGN YOUR OWN MONEY.
WHAT WILL IT LOOK LIKE?

TRY SOME COINS, TOO!

DON'T FORGET TO DESIGN THE BACK

"TO DOODLE OR NOT TO DOODLE: THAT IS THE QUESTION." (ANSWER: DOODLE)
—WILLIAM SHAKESPEARE

I AM CONSIDERED THE GREATEST AUTHOR IN THE ENGLISH LANGUAGE AND THE MOST FAMOUS PLAYWRIGHT IN THE WORLD! I WAS BORN IN ENGLAND MORE THAN 400 YEARS AGO. I WROTE 38 PLAYS AND 154 SONNETS (SONNETS ARE A TYPE OF POEM). I AM THE AUTHOR OF THE PLAY *ROMEO AND JULIET*, THE MOST FAMOUS LOVE STORY OF ALL TIME.

WRITE YOUR OWN
LOVE LETTER

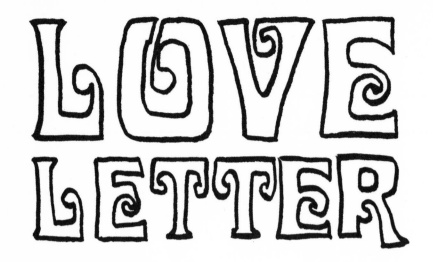

IT CAN BE TO A PARENT, FRIEND, TEACHER, OR TO YOUR VERY OWN ROMEO OR JULIET!

CUT IT OUT OF THE BOOK ALONG THE PERFORATED LINE AND DELIVER IT.

ink

FROM THE DESK OF

_____

(YOUR NAME HERE)

ROMEO NEEDS A HAT

WHAT KIND OF HAT
WILL YOU DRAW FOR HIM?

THE COOL GUY

THE JESTER

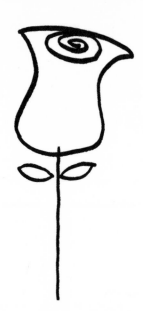

"THAT WHICH WE CALL A ROSE BY ANY OTHER NAME WOULD SMELL AS SWEET."

SYMBOLISM OF ROSES:
ROSES ARE OFTEN USED AS A SYMBOL OF LOVE. SOMETIMES THEY SYMBOLIZE OTHER THINGS, TOO. IN BRITISH HISTORY, THE RED ROSE REPRESENTS THE HOUSE OF LANCASTER.

DRAW A BOUQUET OF ROSES.

PLAN A MASQUERADE BALL— YOU'LL NEED AN INVITE!

WHO'S THAT?
A MASQUERADE BALL

June 2   8:00 p.m.
Will's House

masks required!

YOU CAN DESIGN A LOGO FOR YOUR BALL!

AND A PLAYFUL NAME

DON'T FORGET IMPORTANT STUFF LIKE DATE, TIME, AND LOCATION

MENTION SPECIAL STUFF LIKE "MASKS REQUIRED!"

THE MASQUERADE BALL:
A MASQUERADE BALL IS LIKE A COSTUME PARTY WHERE GUESTS COME WEARING COSTUMES AND MASKS. MASQUERADE BALLS WERE POPULAR IN SHAKESPEARE'S TIME.

DESIGN YOUR OWN INVITATION HERE.

PHOTOCOPY AS MANY COPIES AS YOU NEED. CUT THEM OUT
AND DELIVER THEM TO YOUR FRIENDS.

FANCY IT UP!

ADD SOME BORDERS:

AND SOME EYE-CATCHING
(OR EYE-MASKING!) ART:

IF YOU WANT TO KEEP TRACK
OF HOW MANY PEOPLE WILL
COME TO YOUR BALL, MAKE
A REPLY CARD FOR EACH
GUEST TO RETURN TO YOU,
TELLING YOU WHETHER OR
NOT THEY WILL BE COMING.

MAKE
YOUR OWN
MASK

COLOR OR DOODLE PATTERNS ON THE
MASKS ON THE NEXT FEW PAGES.
DECORATE THEM HOWEVER YOU WOULD LIKE.
CUT THEM OUT AND PUNCH OUT THE
SMALL HOLE ON EACH SIDE. THREAD WITH
ELASTIC OR RIBBON AND YOU CAN
WEAR THEM TO YOUR OWN PARTY!

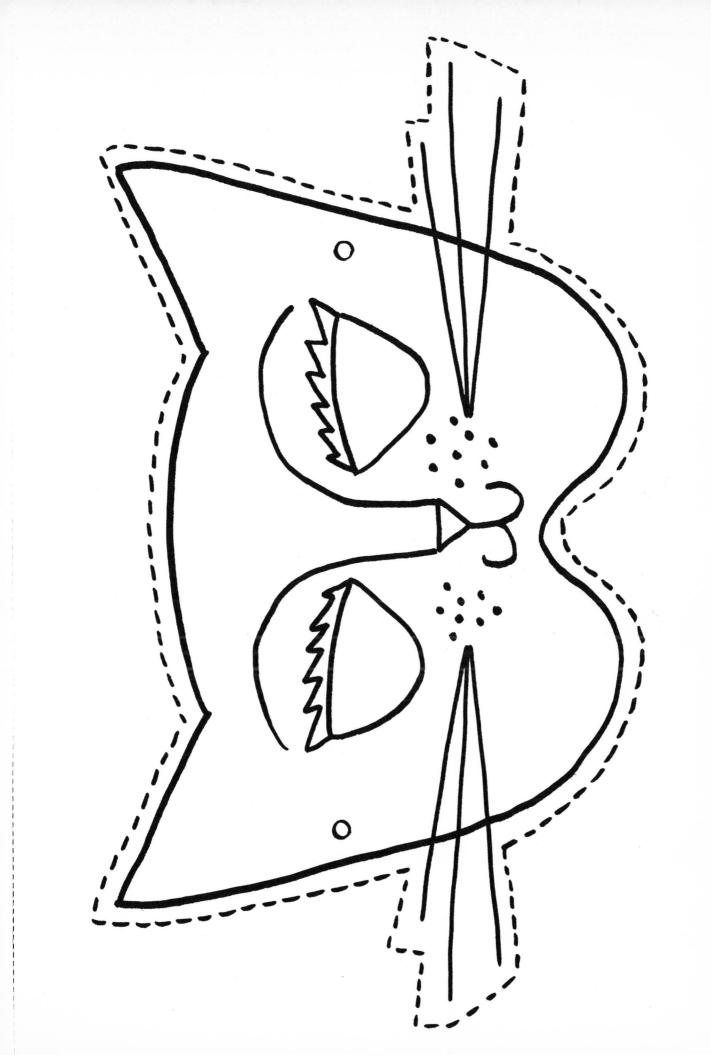

I LOVE YOU, YEAH, YEAH, YEAH

THIS MUSICIAN IS PLAYING A SONG THAT ROMEO IS SINGING TO JULIET. WRITE YOUR OWN WORDS TO THE SONG.

COAT OF ARMS

A COAT OF ARMS IS A DESIGN THAT REPRESENTS A SPECIFIC FAMILY, GROUP OF PEOPLE, OR PLACE. IN SHAKESPEARE'S TIME AND EARLIER, A COAT OF ARMS MIGHT APPEAR ON A SHIELD, A FLAG, OR A PIECE OF CLOTHING. HERE IS THE COAT OF ARMS FOR THE CITY OF VERONA. DRAW A COAT OF ARMS FOR YOUR CITY OR YOUR FAMILY.

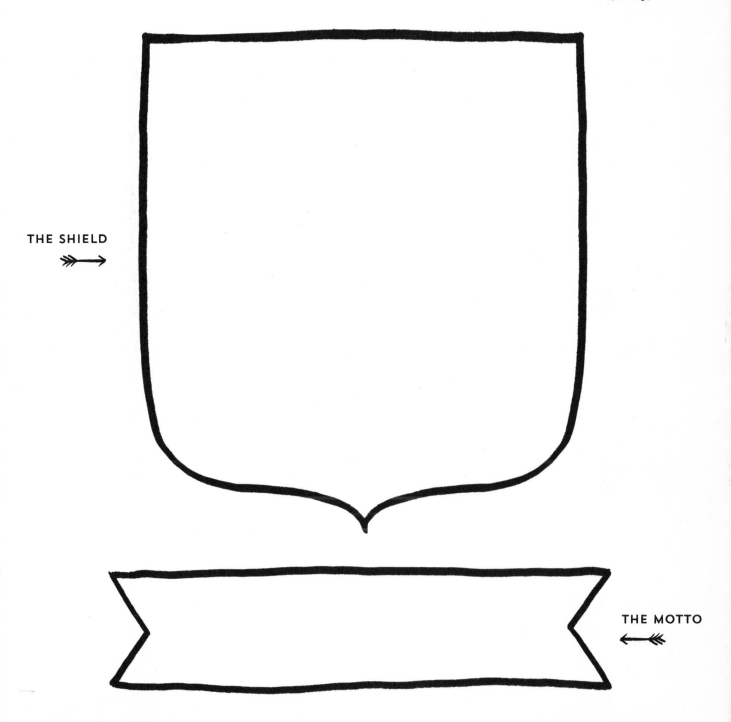

THE CREST
GOES HERE
(LIKE VERONA'S
CROWN)
←⋘

THE SHIELD
⟫→

THE MOTTO
←⋘

 HISTORICAL FOOTNOTE

COATS OF ARMS:

KNIGHTS IN MEDIEVAL TIMES USED COATS OF ARMS TO PROTECT THEM (ON THEIR SHIELDS AND ARMOR) AND TO SHOW WHOSE TEAM THEY FOUGHT ON.

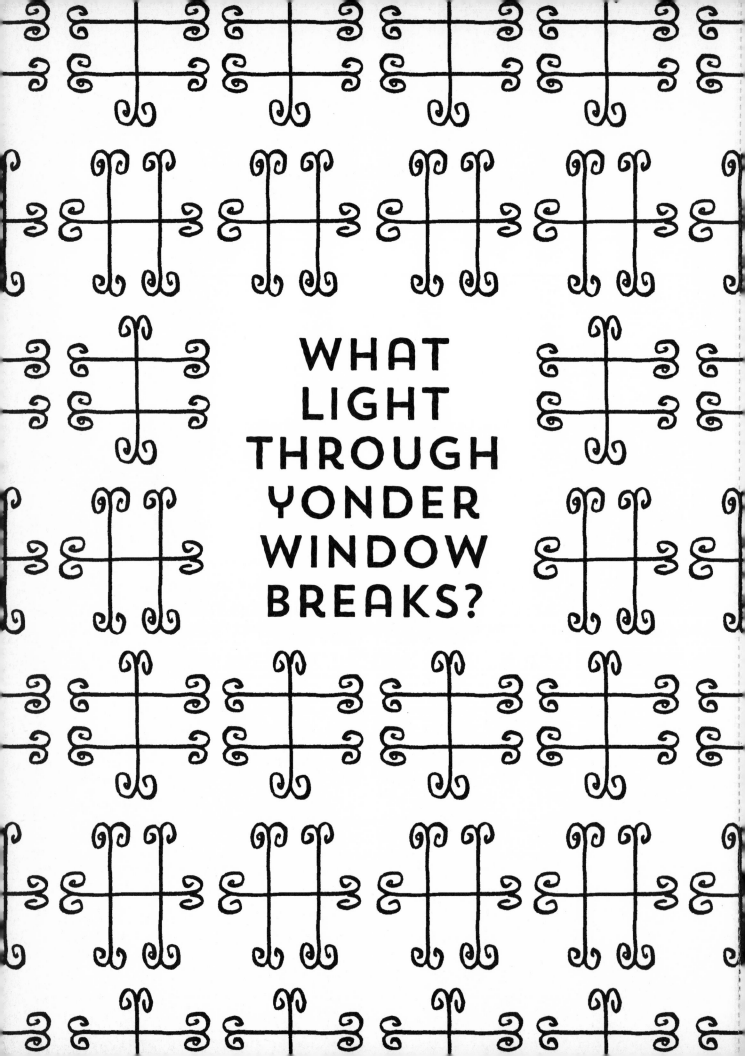

WHAT
LIGHT
THROUGH
YONDER
WINDOW
BREAKS?

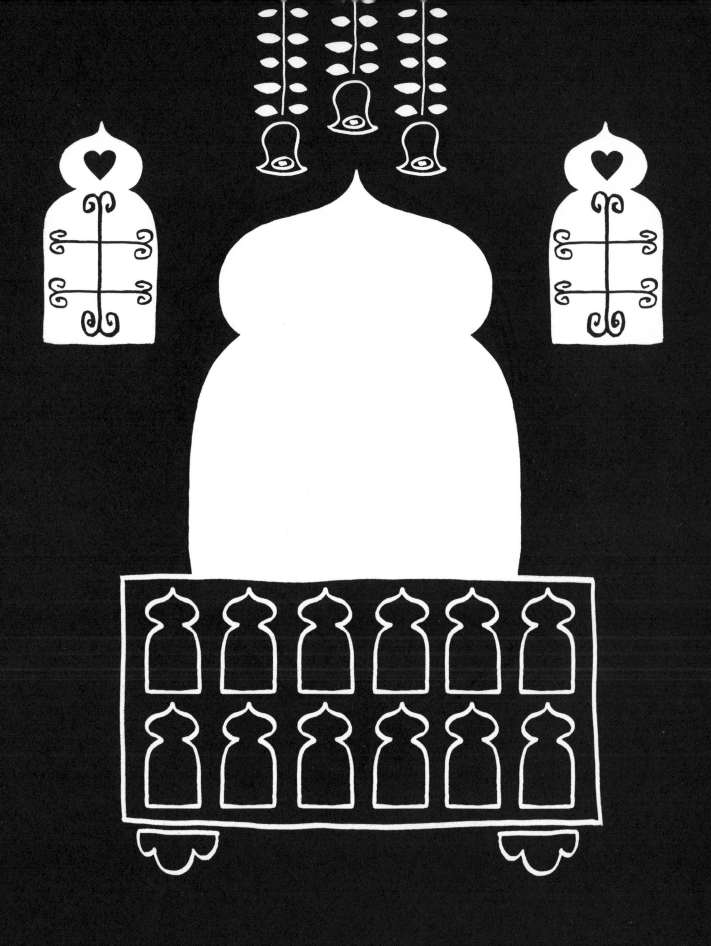

DRAW YOURSELF ON THIS BALCONY.

Yours
faithfully
C Bronte

"I HAVE FOR THE FIRST TIME FOUND WHAT I CAN TRULY LOVE—DOODLING."
—CHARLOTTE BRONTË

I WAS BORN IN 1816 IN ENGLAND AND LIVED IN HAWORTH, A LITTLE TOWN SURROUNDED BY HILLS AND OPEN MOORS. I LIVED WITH MY SISTERS, ANNE AND EMILY, WHO WERE BOTH WRITERS TOO. I AM MOST FAMOUS FOR MY NOVEL *JANE EYRE*.

THE BRONTË SISTERS KEPT EACH OTHER ENTERTAINED BY DRAWING THINGS LIKE THIS CLASSICAL RUIN. CHARLOTTE'S MANUSCRIPTS ARE SCATTERED WITH SKETCHES AND WATERCOLORS.

DECORATE YOUR OWN TRUNK

PUT YOUR INITIALS (ALSO CALLED A "MONOGRAM") ON IT!

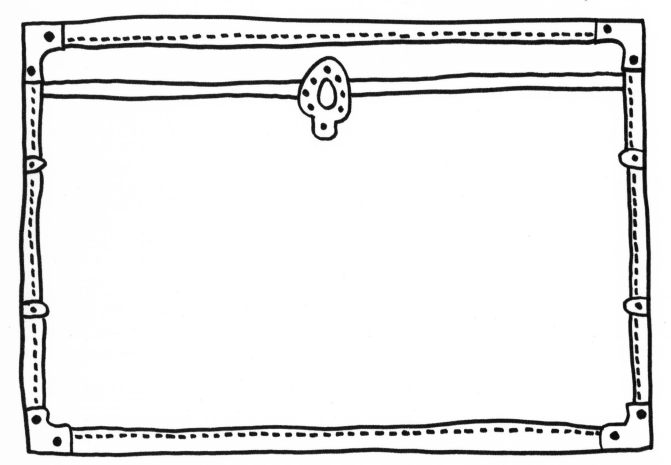

ADD SOME TRAVEL STICKERS OF PLACES YOU'D LIKE TO VISIT

NINETEENTH-CENTURY TRAVEL:

HORSE-DRAWN CARRIAGES OR COACHES WERE USED FOR TRAVEL IN THE NINETEENTH CENTURY.

DRAW ALL THE ITEMS YOU WOULD PACK IN YOUR TRUNK.

BE A BRONTË

FINISH THESE STORIES ON THE CHALKBOARD WITH
A WHITE PENCIL, WITE-OUT PEN, OR SILVER PEN.

"ONE DARK NIGHT IT BEGAN
TO RAIN AND..."

"IN THE MIDDLE OF THE NIGHT,
THE CURTAINS CAUGHT ON FIRE..."

"PILOT WAS A LARGE AND LAZY DOG.
ONE DAY HE..."

NIGHT LIGHTS

"IT IS ALWAYS DANGEROUS TO KEEP A CANDLE LIT AT NIGHT."
—JANE EYRE

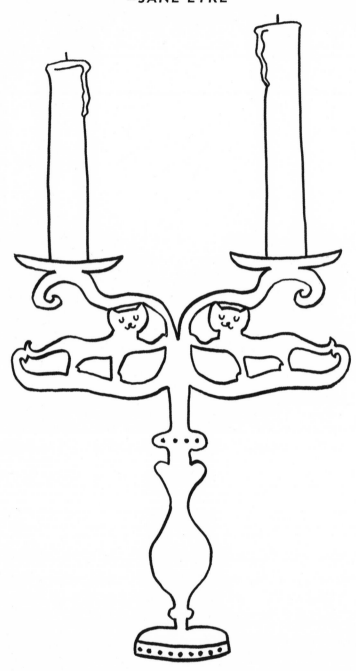

CANDLELIGHTS:
BEFORE ELECTRICITY, PEOPLE LIT THEIR HOMES WITH CANDLES. CANDLES WERE MADE OF TALLOW (THE FAT OF SHEEP OR COWS) OR BEESWAX.

DESIGN A PAIR OF CANDLESTICKS
OR A CANDELABRA.*

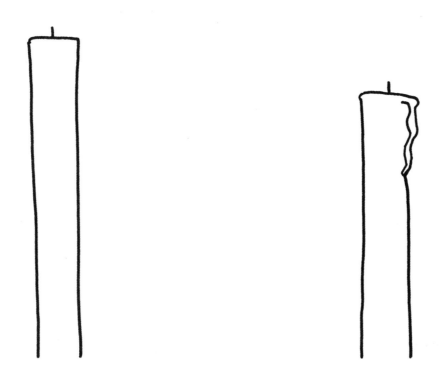

FILL THESE
ARABESQUES*
WITH OBJECTS
OR SHAPES

AN ARABESQUE IS
AN ORNAMENTAL DESIGN
WITH INTERTWINED,
FLOWING LINES.

DEEP IN THE FOREST

DOODLE LEAVES AND BLOSSOMS ON THE TREES ON THE NEXT PAGE. ADD BIRDS AND ANIMALS IN THE FOREST.

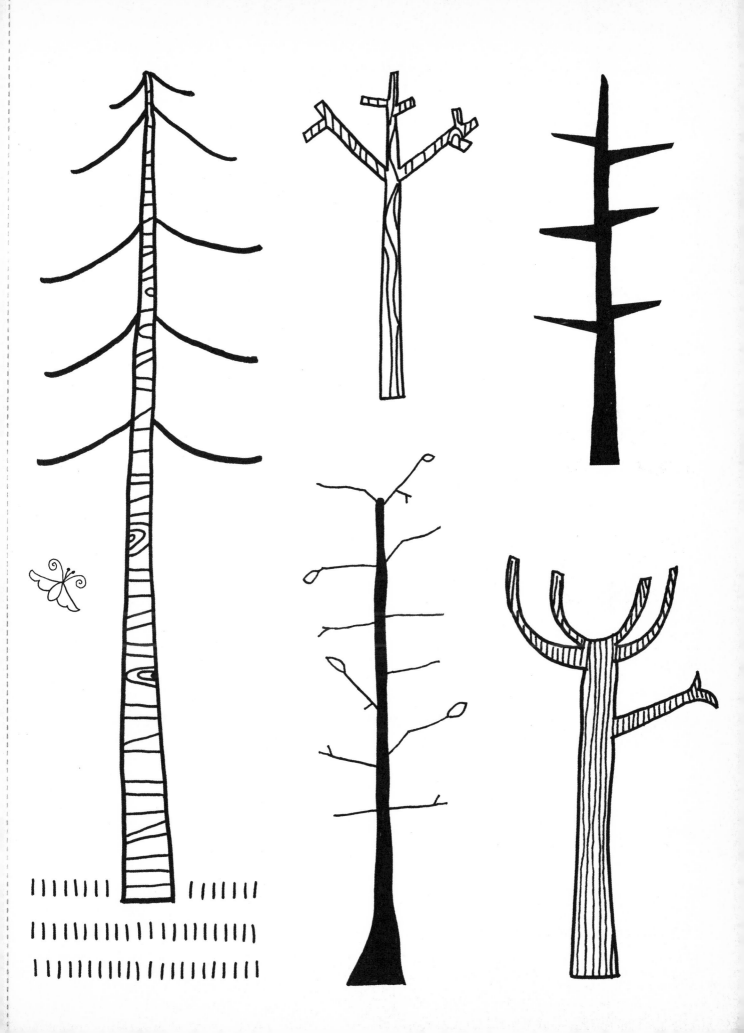

LIFE DRAWINGS

THESE ARE ILLUSTRATIONS FROM JANE EYRE'S LIFE. DOODLE PICTURES FROM YOUR OWN LIFE ON THE NEXT PAGE.

THIS IS PILOT, MR. ROCHESTER'S DOG—DON'T FORGET YOUR PETS!

DESIGN YOUR OWN JEWELRY

HISTORICAL FOOTNOTE

JEWELRY:
THE WORD "JEWELRY" COMES FROM THE LATIN WORD "JOCALE," WHICH MEANS "PLAYTHING."

DRAW A NECKLACE, A BRACELET,
AND EARRINGS.

ENTOMOLOGY IS FUN!
ENTOMOLOGY IS THE STUDY OF INSECTS

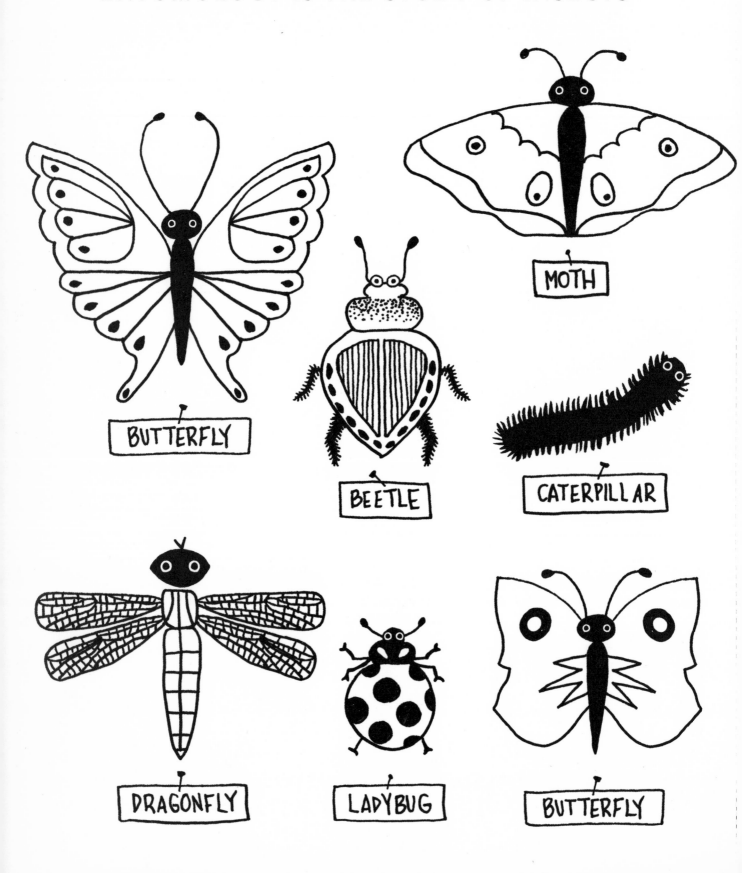

BUTTERFLY

MOTH

BEETLE

CATERPILLAR

DRAGONFLY

LADYBUG

BUTTERFLY

DRAW AND LABEL YOUR OWN INSECTS AND
BUTTERFLIES—BE CREATIVE WITH THEIR NAMES!

DECORATE

MAKE AS MANY PHOTOCOPIES OF THE
FACING PAGE AS YOU LIKE, THEN COLOR
AND DOODLE ON THE PIECES AND CUT
THEM OUT. DECORATE THE BACK SIDES TOO!
HAVE AN ADULT HELP YOU STRING THEM
TOGETHER USING A NEEDLE AND THREAD
TO MAKE YOUR OWN GARLAND.

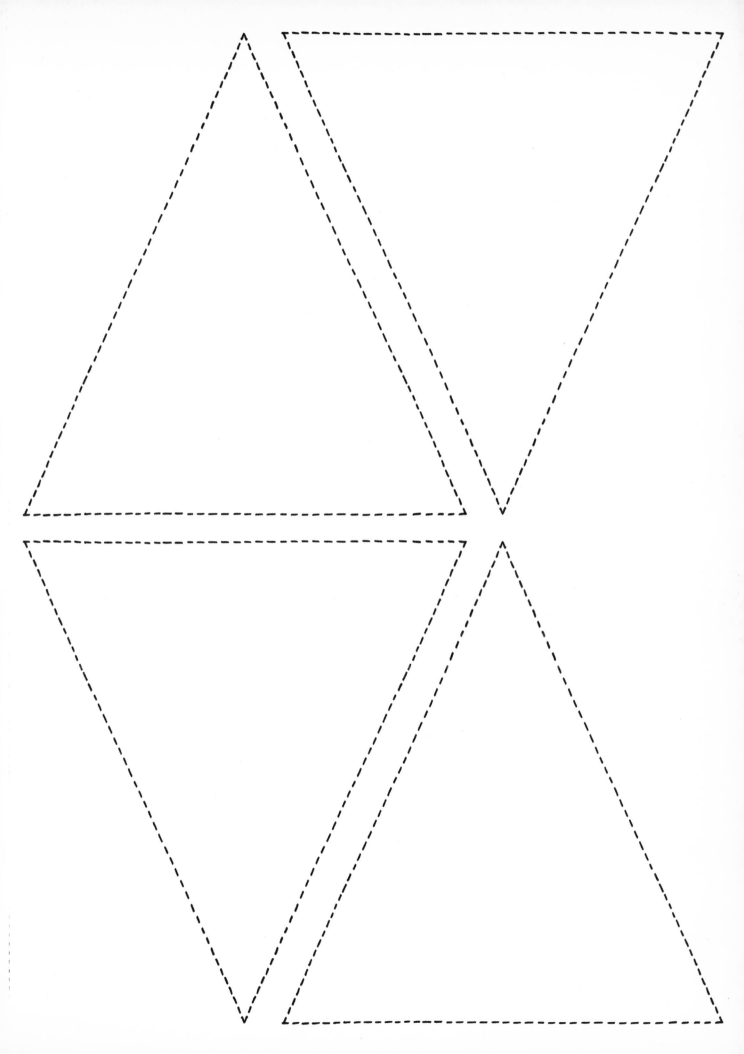

WHAT'S IN YOUR LIBRARY?

FILL IN THE BOOKS ON THIS SHELF.

REPEAT THIS DESIGN
DOWN THE SPINE

WHAT ARE
THE TITLES?

HOW WILL
YOU DECORATE
THE SPINES?

> **"EVERYTHING IS FUNNY, IF YOU CAN DOODLE IT."**
> —LEWIS CARROLL

MY REAL NAME IS CHARLES LUTWIDGE DODGSON. I WAS AN ENGLISH WRITER, MATHEMATICIAN, AND PHOTOGRAPHER. I'M ESPECIALLY WELL KNOWN FOR MY BOOKS *ALICE'S ADVENTURES IN WONDERLAND* AND *THROUGH THE LOOKING-GLASS*, AND THE POEM "JABBERWOCKY."

LEWIS CARROLL'S DOODLES WERE LIKE THESE. ADD MORE THINGS THAT HE MIGHT DOODLE.

WHAT DOES ALICE FIND DOWN THE RABBIT HOLE?

DRAW IT.

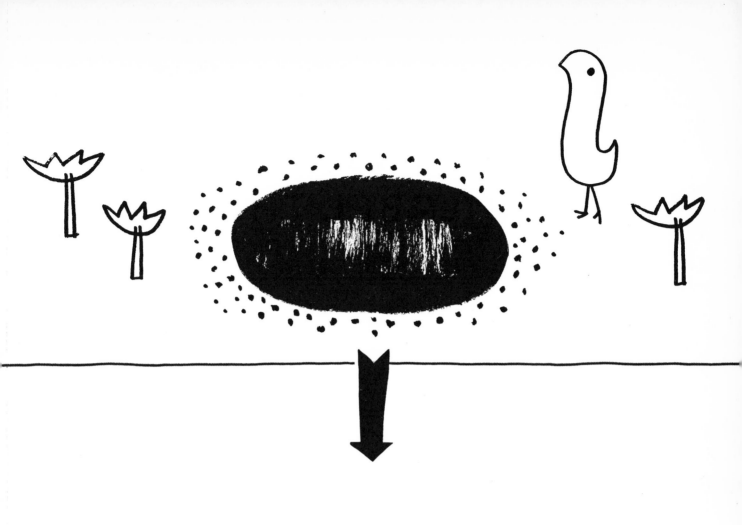

COLOR THE POTIONS IN THE BOTTLES AND LABEL THEM.

SIDE EFFECTS INCLUDE:

THE POTION IN *ALICE IN WONDERLAND* MAKES THE DRINKER GROW SMALLER.

WHAT DO THE POTIONS IN THESE BOTTLES DO?

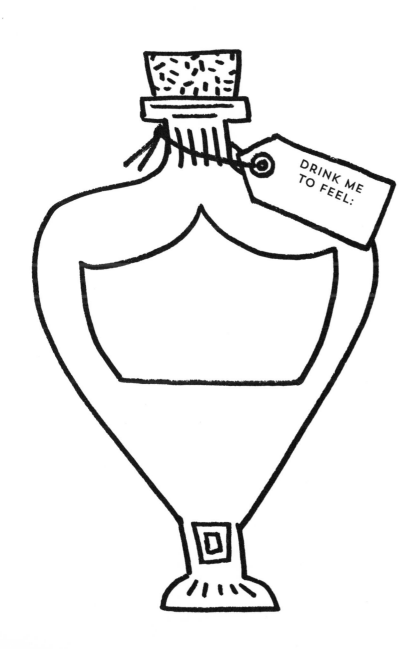

DRINK ME TO FEEL:

DESIGN YOUR OWN
BOTTLE HERE

MAD HATTER MADNESS!

IT COSTS WHAT?!
PUT A PRICE ON
THIS TAG

* MILLINER: A PERSON WHO DESIGNS AND
MAKES HATS IS CALLED A MILLINER.

THE MAD HATTER NEEDS SOME NEW HATS.
DOODLE DIFFERENT HATS FOR HIM.

IT'S A MUSTACHE PARTY!

COLOR THE MUSTACHES AND
CUT THEM OUT. GLUE OR TAPE
THEM TO CRAFT STICKS.
TAKE PICTURES WITH YOUR
FRIENDS SPORTING A MUSTACHE!

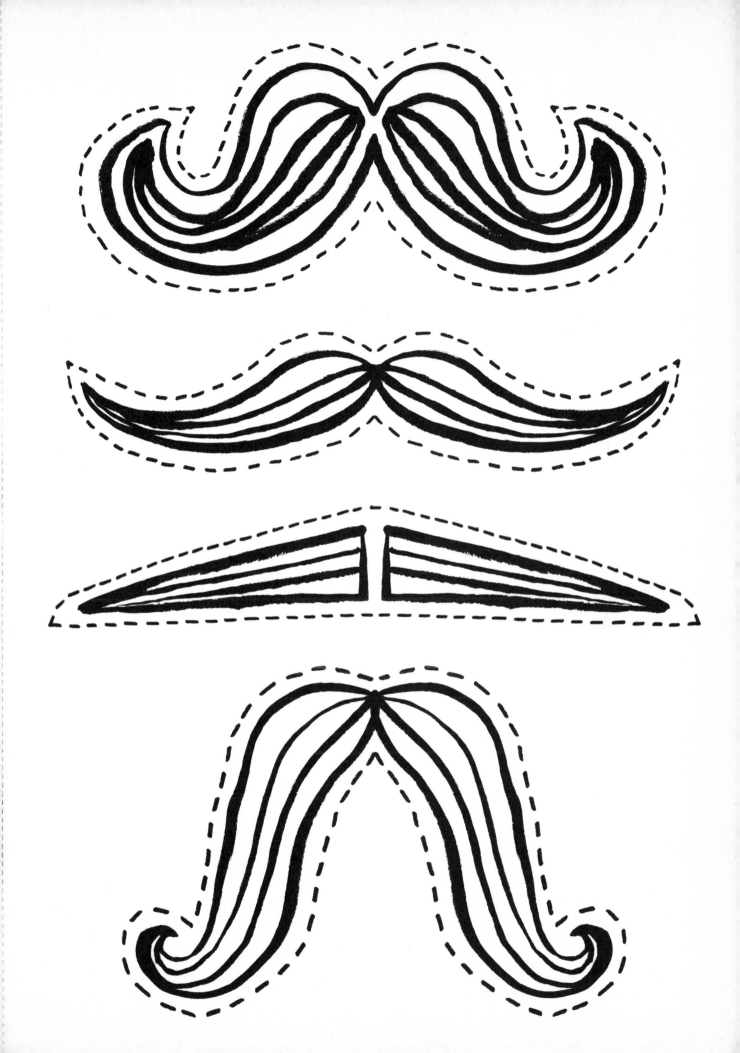

COLORFUL CHARACTERS

COLOR THESE AND DOODLE SOME MORE.

BE THE QUEEN
OF EVERYTHING
(BUT DON'T BE MEAN!)

IF YOU WERE
THE QUEEN,
WHAT WOULD THE
RULES IN YOUR
QUEENDOM BE?

THE RULES

1. _____

2. _____

3. _____

4. _____

5. _____

6. _____

7. _____

8. _____

9. _____

10. _____

WHAT DOES YOUR GARDEN GROW?

THE QUEEN OF HEARTS LIKES
RED ROSES ON HER TREES.
WHAT WOULD YOU LIKE
TO GROW ON YOUR TREES?
DOODLE IT.

QUEEN VICTORIA:

QUEEN VICTORIA WAS ONE OF THE MOST
FAMOUS AND POPULAR QUEENS OF ENGLAND.
SHE WAS QUEEN FROM 1837 UNTIL 1901.
THIS IS CALLED "THE VICTORIAN ERA."

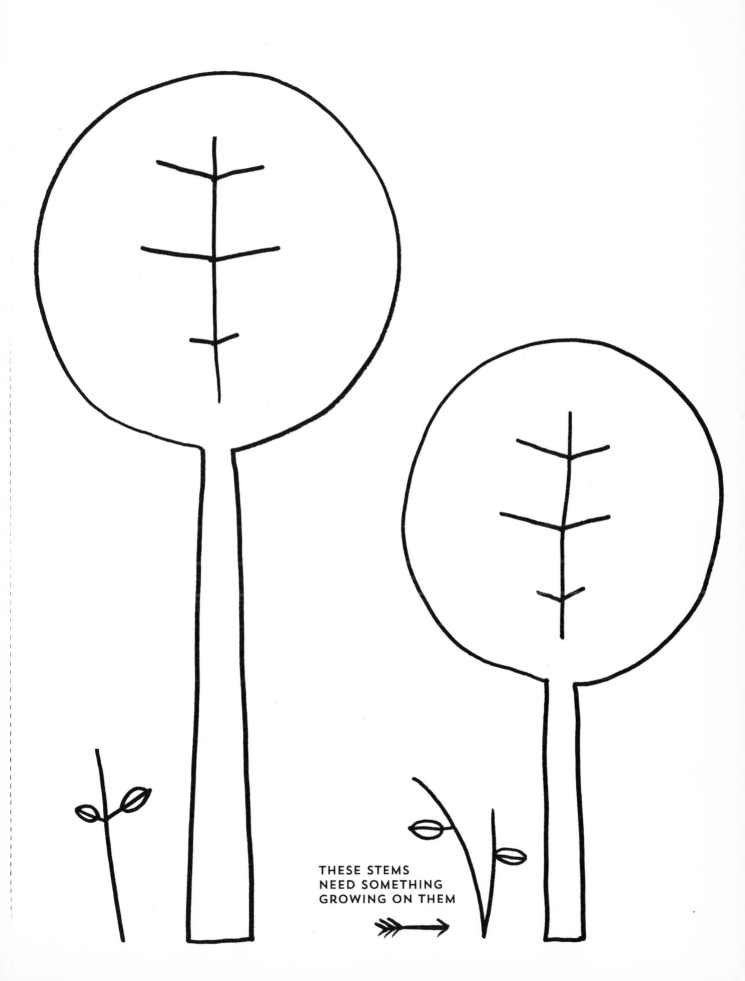

THESE STEMS
NEED SOMETHING
GROWING ON THEM

IT'S TEA PARTY TIME!

PLAN A TEA PARTY.
WHO WILL YOU INVITE?
WHAT FOOD WILL YOU SERVE?

USE THE TEAPOT
ILLUSTRATION AS
AN INVITATION.

MAKE AS MANY
PHOTOCOPIES OF THIS
PAGE AS YOU NEED.
PHOTOCOPY ONTO
CARD STOCK FOR A
STURDIER INVITATION.

DOODLE DIFFERENT DESIGNS ON
THE INVITATIONS. GO CRAZY! COLOR THEM
WITH CRAYONS OR MARKERS, PAINT THEM,
OR USE GLUE AND GLITTER. CUT THEM
OUT AND WRITE THE DETAILS OF
YOUR PARTY ON THE BACK.
DELIVER THEM TO YOUR FRIENDS.

I, FROG FOOTMAN
A LIFE IN GREEN

BY

_____

WRITE THE LIFE STORY
OF FROG FOOTMAN.

WHITE RABBIT LOVES TWO THINGS: BEING ON TIME AND AWESOME TEES

DESIGN NEW LOGOS FOR WHITE RABBIT'S T-SHIRTS.

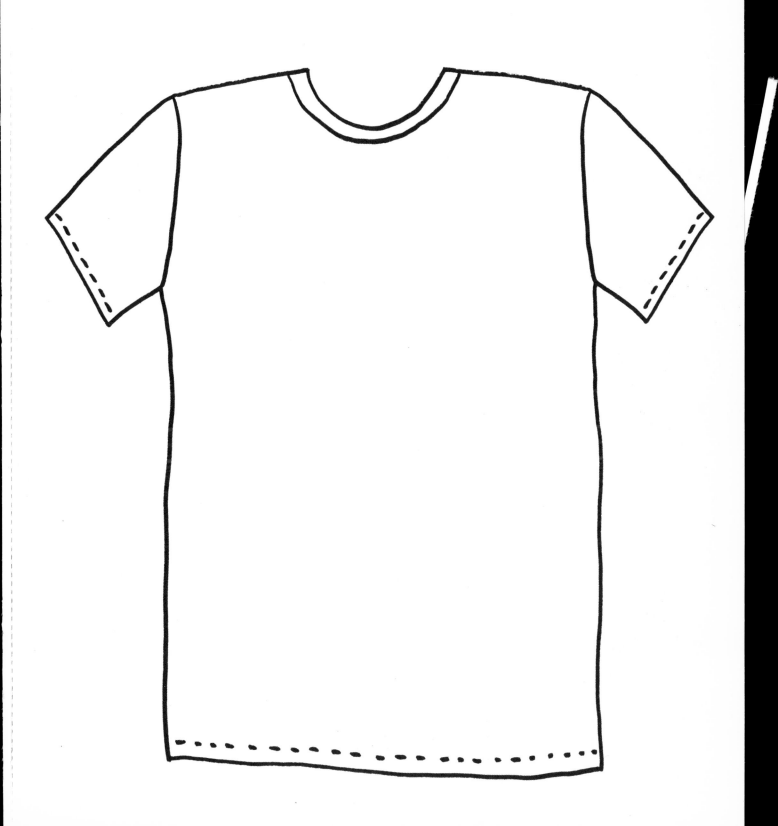

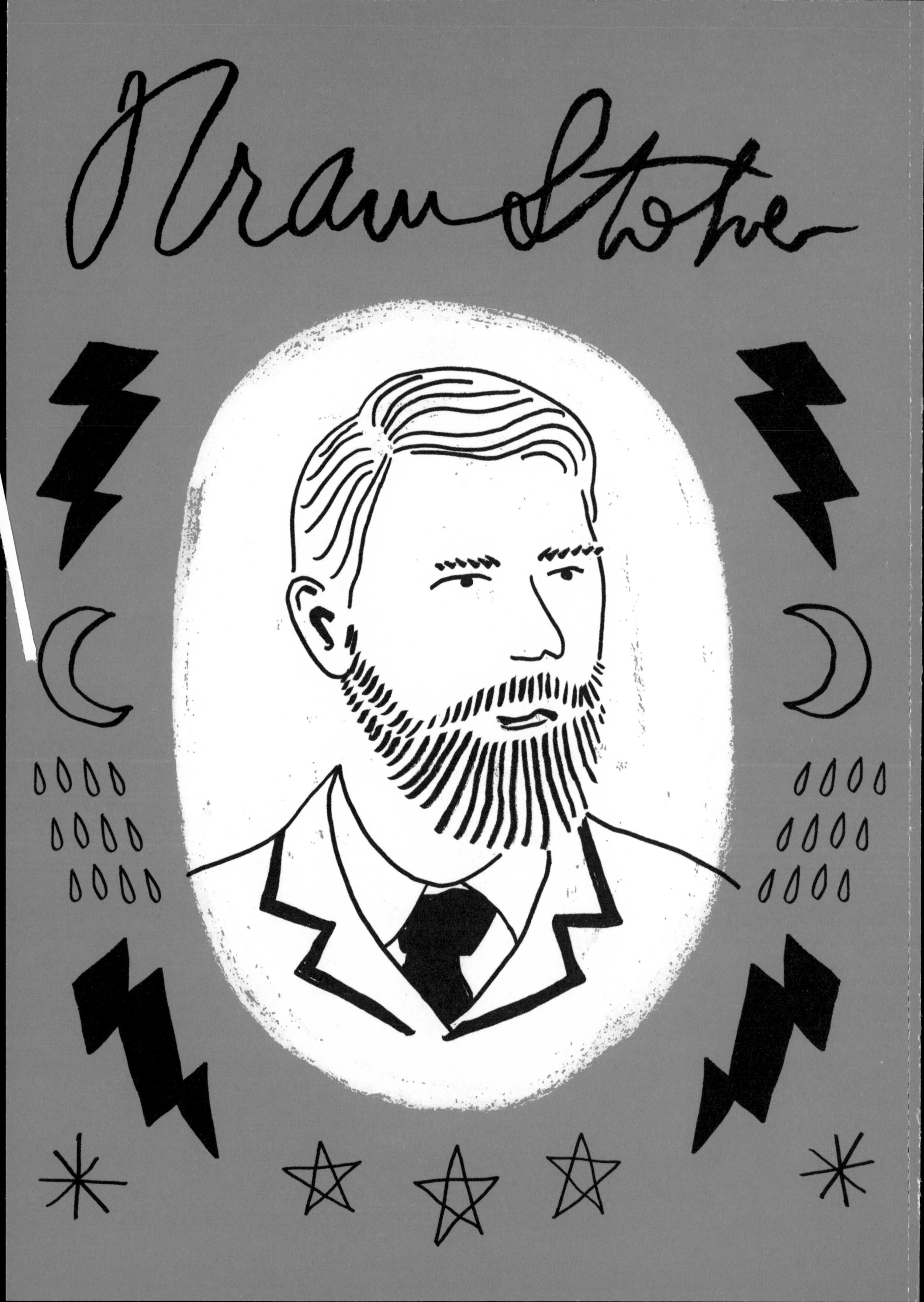
Bram Stoker

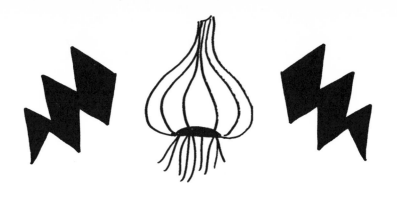

"DOODLING HAS ITS OWN CALMS."
—BRAM STOKER

I WAS BORN IN DUBLIN, IRELAND, IN 1847. "BRAM" IS SHORT FOR "ABRAHAM." I WORKED AS THE PERSONAL ASSISTANT TO AN ACTOR AND THE BUSINESS MANAGER OF THE LYCEUM THEATRE IN LONDON. I WROTE MORE THAN A DOZEN NOVELS, BUT THE BEST-KNOWN ONE IS *DRACULA*. IT IS ONE OF THE MOST FAMOUS HORROR NOVELS OF ALL TIME AND INFLUENCES HOW PEOPLE THINK ABOUT VAMPIRES TODAY.

A VAMPIRE'S CASTLE

DRACULA LIVES HERE.

DRAW YOUR OWN CASTLE.

STAMP IT

THE CHARACTERS IN *DRACULA* WRITE EACH OTHER LETTERS. DESIGN STAMPS FOR THEM.

THE POSTAGE STAMP:
THE PENNY BLACK WAS THE WORLD'S FIRST POSTAGE STAMP. IT WAS A STAMP IN THE UNITED KINGDOM AND HAD A PICTURE OF QUEEN VICTORIA ON IT. THE FIRST DAY YOU COULD USE IT WAS MAY 6, 1840.

Express!

HOOOOOOOWWWL!

WOLVES HOWL. DRAW THE ANIMALS THAT MAKE THESE OTHER SOUNDS:

DRAW A SHIP ON THE OCEAN.

THESE ARE SOME OF THE HEROES IN *DRACULA*.

VAMPIRES DON'T LIKE GARLIC, SO I WEAR IT ON A NECKLACE.

JONATHAN HARKER   ARTHUR HOLMWOOD   DR. VAN HELSING

DRAW A PICTURE OF YOUR HERO.

_____

(YOUR HERO'S NAME HERE)

BOO!

DESIGN THESE TO REFLECT
YOUR INNER VAMPIRE.

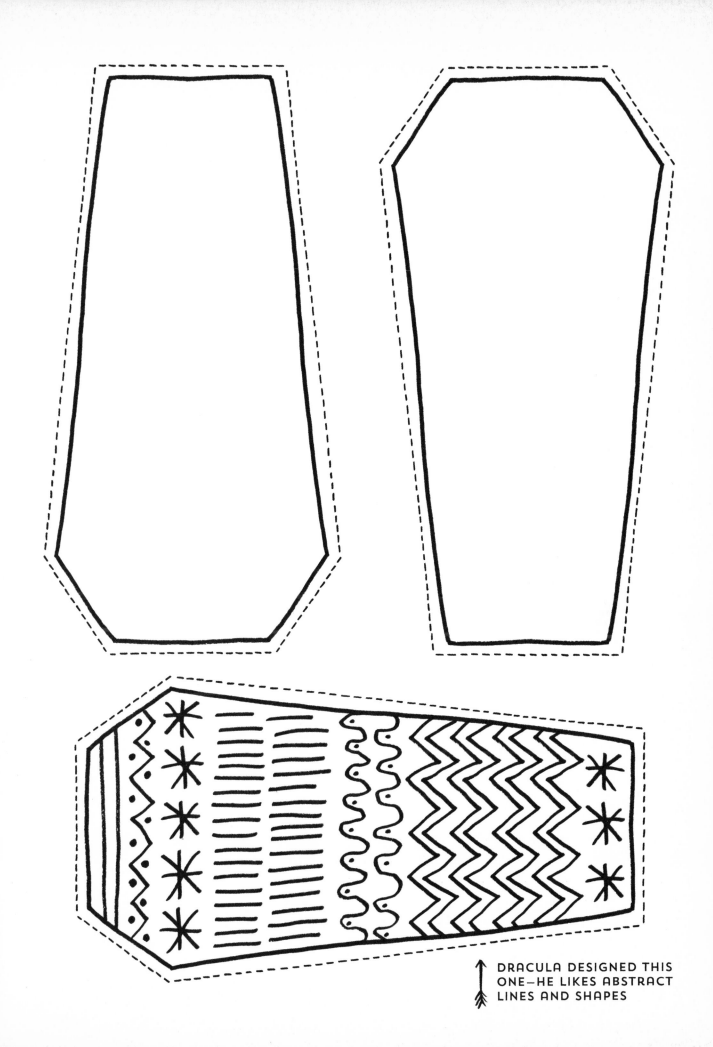

DRACULA DESIGNED THIS
ONE—HE LIKES ABSTRACT
LINES AND SHAPES

DEAR DIARY....

JOURNAL ABOUT YOUR DAY. WHAT WAS
YOUR FAVORITE THING? LEAST FAVORITE THING?
DOODLE SOME OF THE THINGS YOU SAW OR DID.

A VERY LONG TIME AGO, A HUNDRED YEARS OR MORE, A FAMILY OF RATS DECIDED TO TAKE A TRIP FROM _____ TO _____. THEY NEEDED TO
(NAME OF CITY OR COUNTRY)   (NAME OF CITY OR COUNTRY)

_____ , WHICH IS WHY THEY HAD TO TRAVEL. THERE WERE FIVE RATS IN THE FAMILY. THEIR NAMES WERE _____ , _____ , _____ , _____ , AND _____ . _____ WAS LAZY AND LIKED TO SLEEP ALL THE TIME. _____ WAS THE WELL-ORGANIZED ONE—HE WAS GOOD AT PACKING. _____ JUST LIKED TO READ BOOKS. THE DAY BEFORE THEY WERE READY TO GO, _____ GOT THEM ALL PACKED. HE PUT _____ , _____ , _____ , AND _____ IN HIS BACKPACK, WHICH HE KNEW THEY'D NEED ON THEIR JOURNEY. _____ DID A BUNCH OF EXERCISES TO MAKE SURE HE WAS IN SHAPE, AND _____ JUST SLEPT. THAT NIGHT, THEY CREPT TO THE DOCK AND SNEAKED ONTO A SHIP. THEY HEARD THE SHIP CREAK AND MOAN, AND HEARD THE WATER LAPPING AGAINST THE SIDES. THEY STOWED AWAY CAREFULLY BELOW DECK. ABOUT MIDNIGHT, THE CAPTAIN ORDERED THE SHIP TO SET SAIL. THEN _____

_____ . . .

BLUE IS THE NEW BLACK

DRACULA IS SO BORED WITH HIS CAPE.
I MEAN, HE'S BEEN WEARING IT
FOR LIKE 450 YEARS.

COLOR THIS NEW CAPE, THEN CUT IT OUT AND PASTE IT OVER DRACULA'S OLD CAPE.

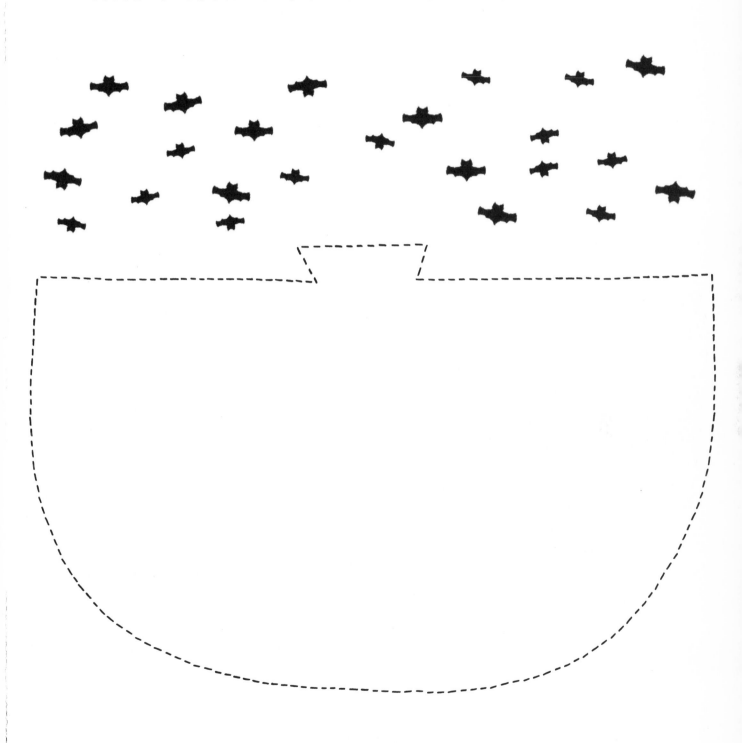

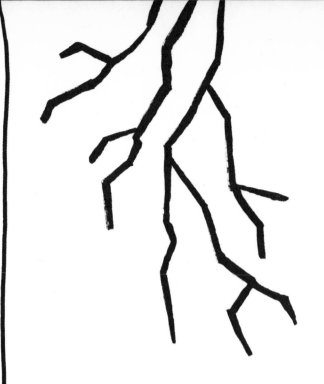

DRACULA'S FOREST

DOODLE DESIGNS ON THESE TREE TRUNKS.

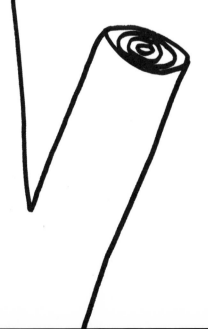

Herman Melville

"DOODLING AT FIRST SIGHT, LIKE LOVE AT FIRST SIGHT, IS SAID TO BE THE ONLY TRUTH."
—HERMAN MELVILLE

I WROTE *MOBY-DICK*, WHICH IS ABOUT SAILORS WHO CATCH WHALES AT SEA. MANY PEOPLE CALL IT THE GREAT AMERICAN NOVEL. I WORKED ON A WHALING BOAT MYSELF. I WAS A SUCCESSFUL WRITER IN THE BEGINNING OF MY CAREER, BUT MY POPULARITY FADED AND BY THE TIME I DIED IN 1891 NO ONE REMEMBERED ME. THEN, ALMOST 100 YEARS LATER, PEOPLE REMEMBERED WHAT AN IMPORTANT BOOK *MOBY-DICK* IS AND I BECAME FAMOUS AGAIN.

MELVILLE DREW THIS FROM MEMORY WHILE SAILING ON THE *METEOR*. IT IS HIS HOME, ARROWHEAD FARM, WHERE HE FINISHED WRITING *MOBY-DICK*.

BON VOYAGE!
"BON VOYAGE" IS FRENCH FOR "GOOD JOURNEY."

WHAT WOULD YOU PACK IN YOUR DUFFEL BAG FOR AN OCEAN VOYAGE? DOODLE IT.

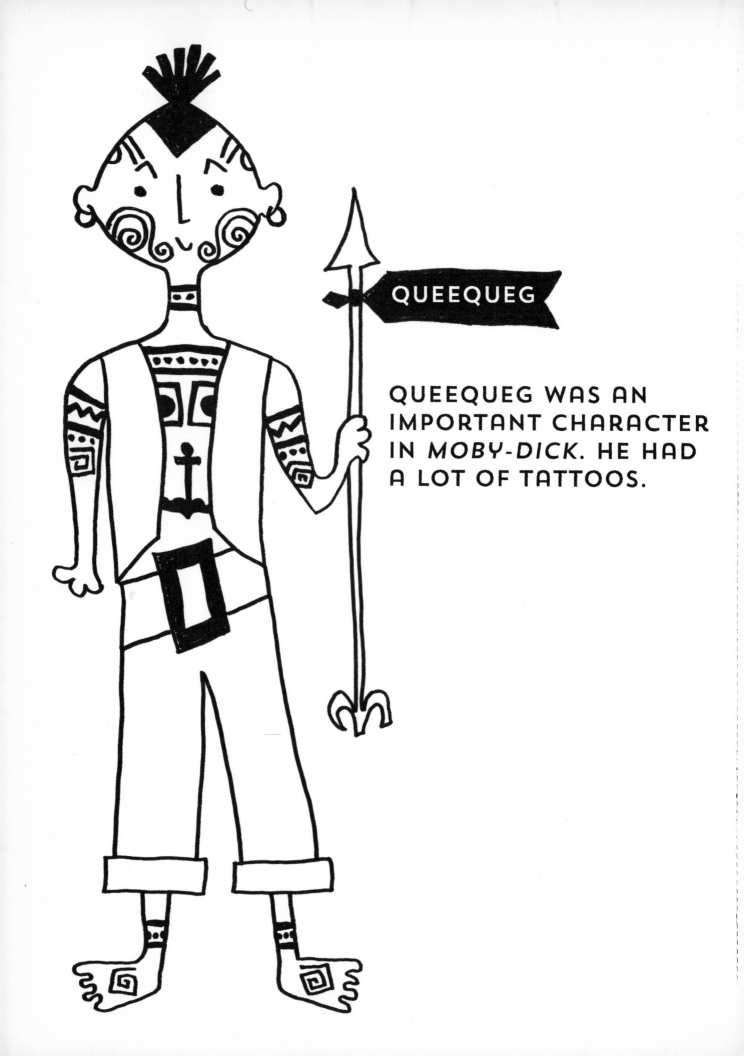

QUEEQUEG

QUEEQUEG WAS AN
IMPORTANT CHARACTER
IN *MOBY-DICK*. HE HAD
A LOT OF TATTOOS.

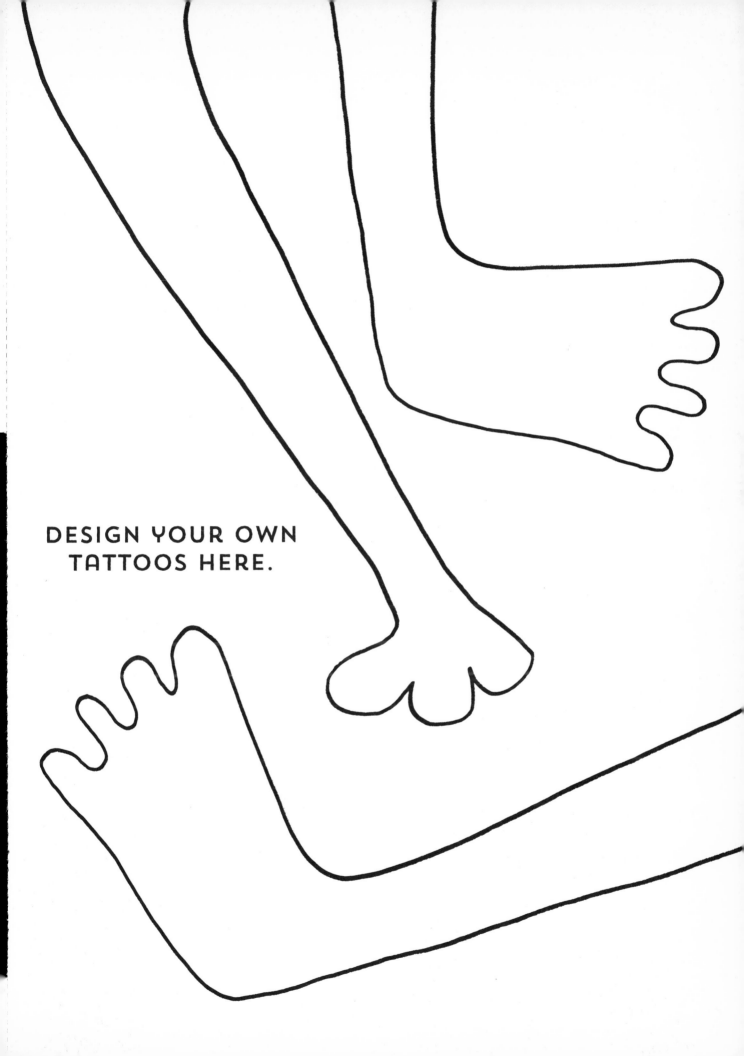

DESIGN YOUR OWN
TATTOOS HERE.

THE ART OF THE HIGH SEAS

THIS IS SCRIMSHAW

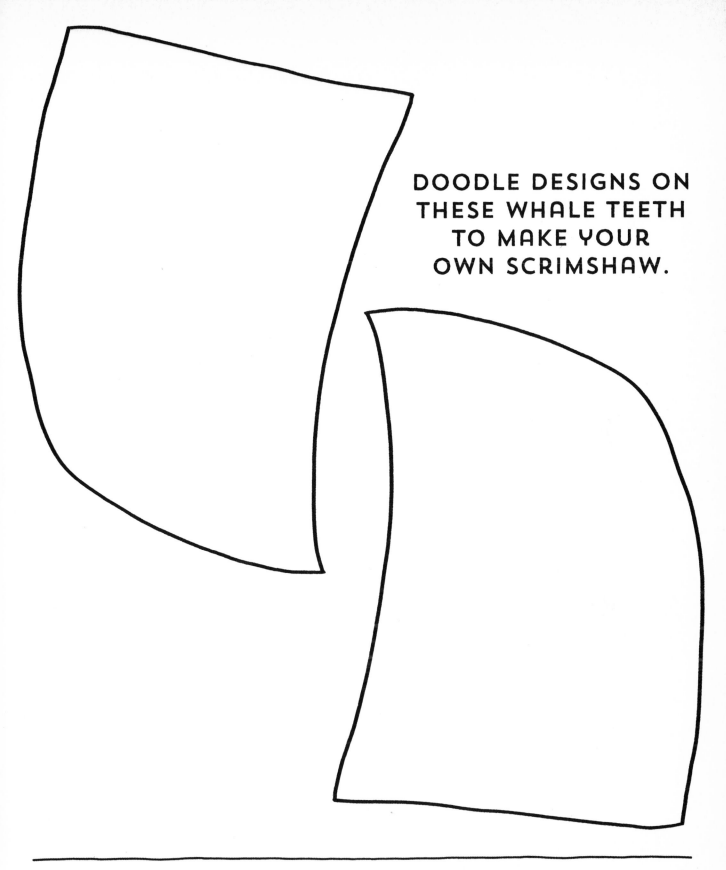

DOODLE DESIGNS ON THESE WHALE TEETH TO MAKE YOUR OWN SCRIMSHAW.

 HISTORICAL FOOTNOTE

SCRIMSHAW:
SCRIMSHAW IS WHAT SAILORS CALLED THE CARVINGS THEY MADE ON THE BONES OR TEETH OF WHALES. SOMETIMES THEY HUNG THEM FROM THE SIDES OF THEIR SHIPS AS DECORATIONS.

SQUAWK!
SQUAWK!

THESE TWO NOISY SEAGULLS NEED A BUDDY.
DRAW ONE IN THE NEST.

IF YOU WERE CAPTAIN, WHAT WOULD THE FLAG FOR YOUR SHIP BE? DESIGN ONE, CUT IT OUT, AND HANG IT IN YOUR ROOM.

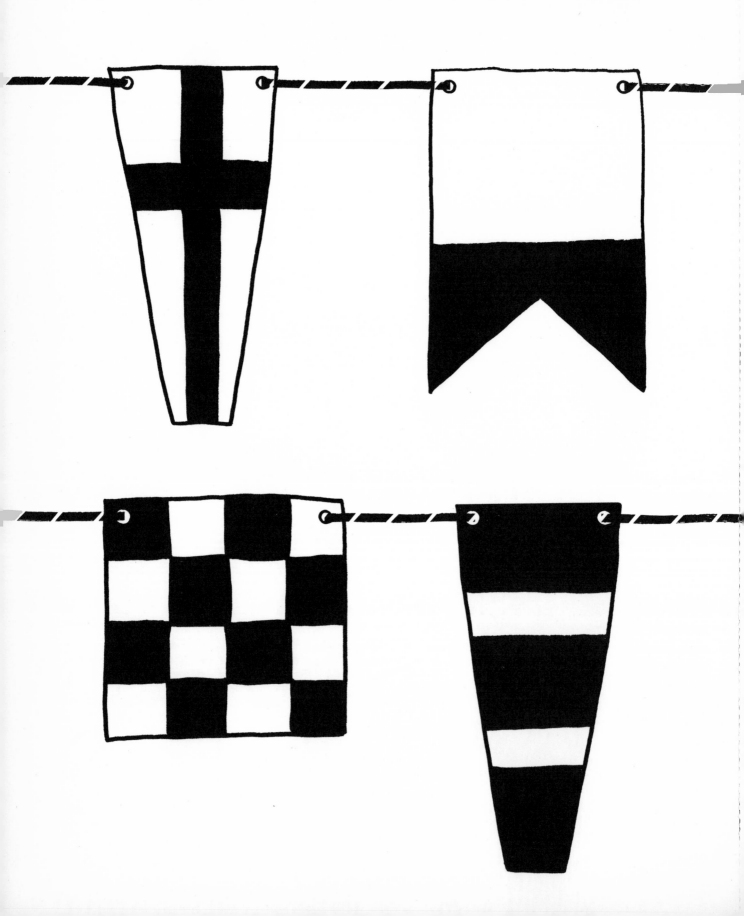

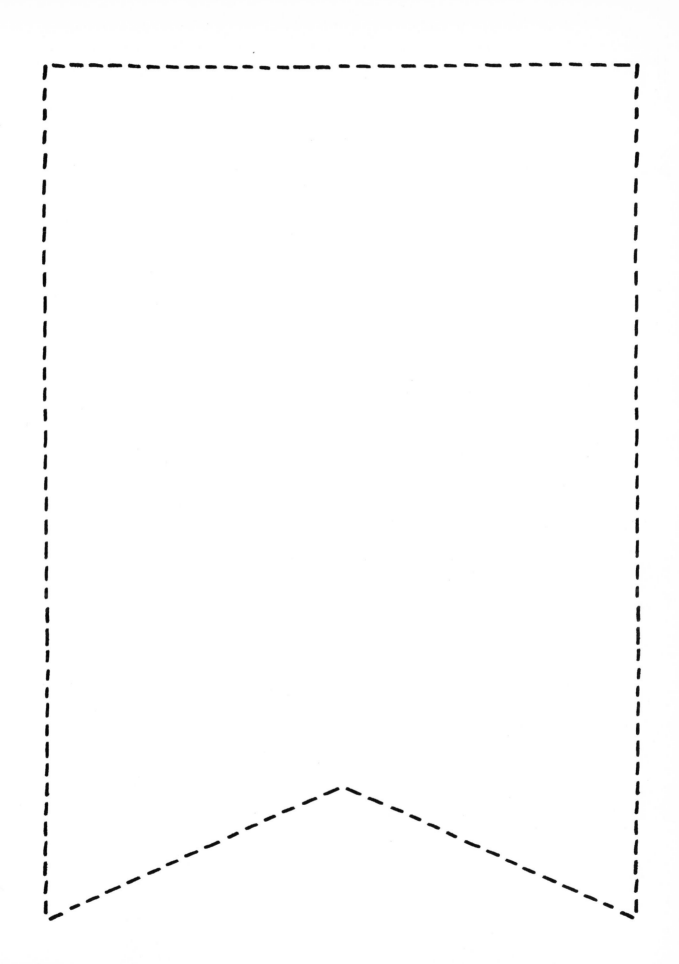

I SPY A CAPTAIN

DRAW THE FACE OF CAPTAIN AHAB
LOOKING THROUGH THE BOAT'S PORTHOLE*.

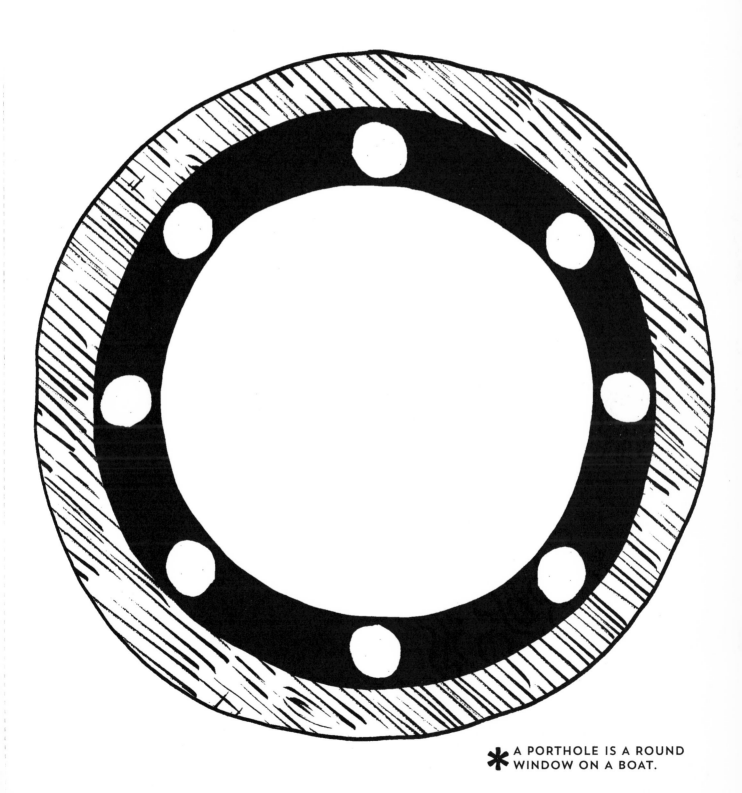

* A PORTHOLE IS A ROUND
WINDOW ON A BOAT.

SWIM WITH
THE FISHES

DOODLE FISH IN THIS OCEAN.

THE WHITE WHALE

MOBY-DICK* IS A VERY MYSTERIOUS WHALE;
HE DOESN'T APPEAR VERY OFTEN.
WHAT DO YOU THINK HE LOOKS LIKE?

COLOR THE HARPOONS AND DOODLE PATTERNS ON THEM.

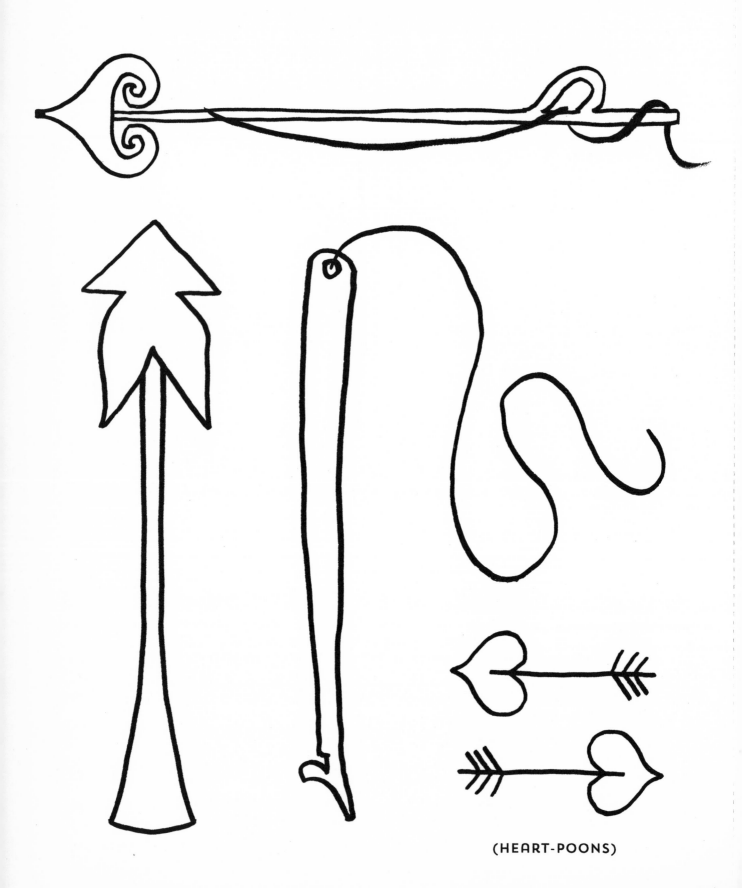

(HEART-POONS)

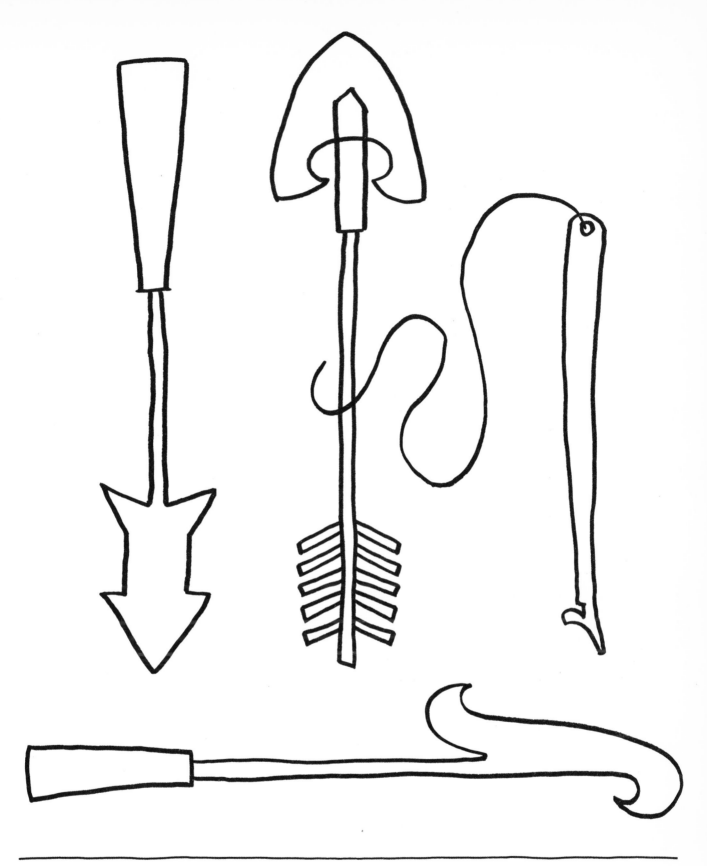

HISTORICAL FOOTNOTE

WHAT IS A HARPOON?

A HARPOON IS A LONG SPEAR THAT FISHERMEN CAN USE TO CATCH FISH OR WHALES.

'NIGHT, 'NIGHT

CONNECT THE STARS TO CREATE YOUR OWN CONSTELLATIONS IN THE NIGHT SKY.

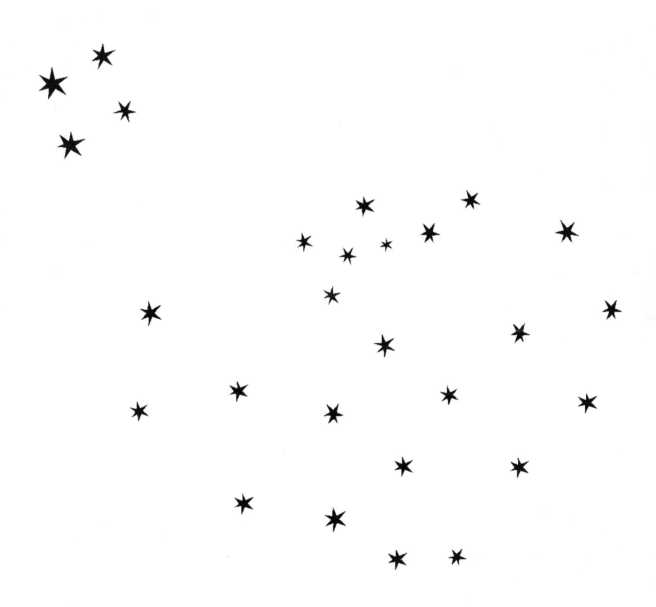

Arthur Conan Doyle.

"THEY SAY THAT GENIUS IS AN INFINITE CAPACITY FOR DOODLING."
–SIR ARTHUR CONAN DOYLE

I WAS BORN ON MAY 22, 1859 IN EDINBURGH, SCOTLAND. AS A YOUNG BOY, I WAS SENT TO BOARDING SCHOOL IN ENGLAND FOR SEVEN YEARS, WHERE I LEARNED THAT I LIKED TO PLAY CRICKET* AND HAD A TALENT FOR STORYTELLING. I INVENTED SHERLOCK HOLMES, THE MOST FAMOUS OF ALL FICTIONAL DETECTIVES. MY BOOKS GREATLY INFLUENCED OTHER DETECTIVE STORIES AND CRIME NOVELS.

* CRICKET IS A POPULAR GAME PLAYED WITH A BAT AND BALL. IT CAN BE TRACED BACK TO TUDOR TIMES IN EARLY SIXTEENTH-CENTURY ENGLAND. THAT'S A LONG TIME AGO!

CONAN DOYLE SERVED AS A SURGEON ON A WHALING SHIP CALLED *HOPE* AND KEPT A DETAILED JOURNAL WITH DRAWINGS OF WHAT HE ENCOUNTERED, LIKE THIS SNOW HOUSE WHICH HE DESCRIBED AS "12-FEET HIGH, SHAPED LIKE A BEEHIVE."

HOW-TO HOUND

FOLLOW THE STEPS TO DRAW A HOUND.

1

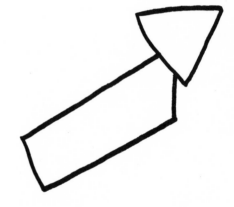

2

ADD SOME EYES,
EARS, AND A NOSE

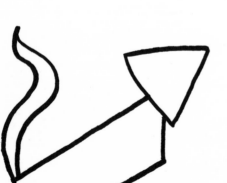

3

4

PUT SOME HOUNDS IN THIS
SPOOKY NIGHT SCENE.

CREEEEEEEEEEAK!

DESIGN YOUR OWN METAL GATES ON THE NEXT PAGE.

DO THESE GARGOYLES*
LOOK LIKE THE HOUNDS
YOU JUST DREW?

* A GARGOYLE IS A CARVED
FACE OR FIGURE MEANT TO
SCARE OFF INTRUDERS.

IF YOU OWNED A SHOE STORE,
WHAT WOULD YOU SELL? FILL THESE
SHELVES WITH BOOTS, SHOES, SLIPPERS,
SANDALS, AND FLIP-FLOPS.

CIRCLES

WHAT CAN YOU DOODLE USING
THIS SHAPE? IS IT A MOTORCYCLE WHEEL?
A DINOSAUR EYE? A PIZZA? DRAW IT.

BE A MICHELANGELO

DRAW A BUST* OF YOURSELF
AND EACH OF YOUR FAMILY MEMBERS.

* A BUST IS A SCULPTURE SHOWING A PERSON'S HEAD, NECK, AND SOMETIMES SHOULDERS. THEY ARE OFTEN MADE OUT OF MARBLE OR BRONZE.

LEAF IT!

GATHER LEAVES FROM OUTSIDE.
GET A REGULAR OR THIN PIECE OF PAPER.
PLACE THE LEAVES UNDER IT IN AN
INTERESTING PATTERN AND WEIGH
DOWN THE CORNERS OF THE PAPER
WITH SOMETHING HEAVY.
USE A PLAIN OR COLORED PENCIL
AND LIGHTLY COLOR OVER THE PAPER
SO THE SHAPES AND LINES SHOW THROUGH.

GLUE OR TAPE THE
PAPER ON THIS PAGE.

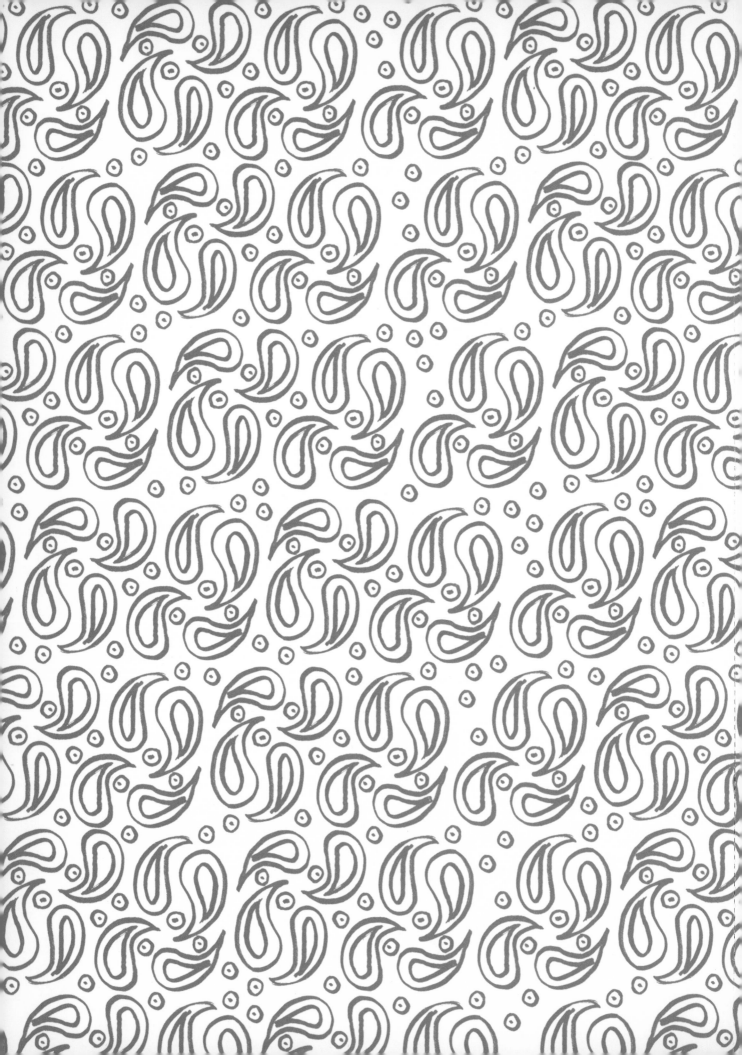

DRAW A FIREPLACE AND MANTEL
AROUND THIS FIRE. MAKE IT AS PLAIN OR
AS FANCY AS YOU WOULD LIKE.

HELLO GARGOYLES!

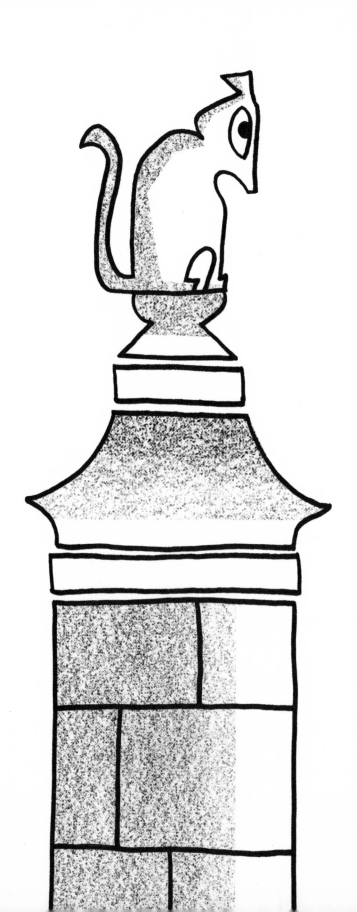

DOODLE DIFFERENT GARGOYLES HERE.
MAKE THEM SCARY!

HATS ON!

DRAW THE HEADS
THAT THESE HATS GO ON.

PATTERNS ARE FUN!

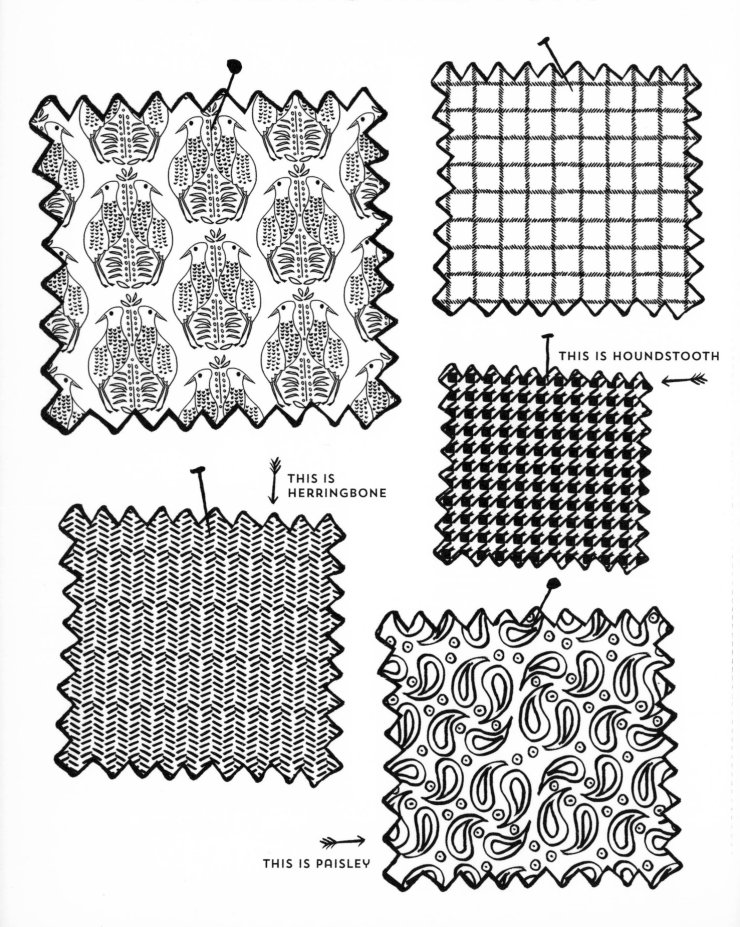

THIS IS HOUNDSTOOTH

THIS IS HERRINGBONE

THIS IS PAISLEY

DOODLE OTHER PATTERNS. HOW ABOUT
POLKA DOT, CHECKERED, OR FLORAL?
WHAT OTHER PATTERNS CAN YOU MAKE?

"HONEST PEOPLE DON'T HIDE THEIR DOODLES."
—EMILY BRONTË

I WROTE UNDER THE NAME "ELLIS BELL." I USED A MAN'S NAME BECAUSE WHEN I WROTE IN THE NINETEENTH CENTURY, IT WASN'T CONSIDERED PROPER FOR WOMEN TO BE AUTHORS! GOOD THING THAT'S CHANGED. I WROTE POETRY, BUT I AM MOST FAMOUS FOR MY NOVEL *WUTHERING HEIGHTS*. IT'S THE LOVE STORY OF TWO CHARACTERS CALLED HEATHCLIFF AND CATHY. IT'S A VERY UNHAPPY STORY BECAUSE HEATHCLIFF AND CATHY WERE NOT NICE TO EACH OTHER.

Emily

THIS IS A SIMPLE SELF-PORTRAIT OF EMILY AT HER DESK WRITING.

MULTIPLE BRONTËS:
EMILY'S SISTER WAS CHARLOTTE BRONTË, WHO WROTE *JANE EYRE*. SHE ALSO HAD A SISTER NAMED ANNE, WHO WROTE A BOOK CALLED *THE TENANT OF WILDFELL HALL*.

SPRING HAS SPRUNG

DOODLE SPRINGTIME LEAVES
AND BLOSSOMS ON THE TREE.
WHAT KIND OF TREE DO
YOU WANT IT TO BE?
WHAT COLOR OF BLOSSOMS
WILL IT HAVE?

 **HISTORICAL FOOTNOTE**

BIRDS ON THE MOORS:
SOME BIRDS THAT LIVE ON THE
MOORS HAVE FUN NAMES, LIKE:
CURLEWS, LAPWINGS, MEADOW PIPITS,
AND WHINCHATS.

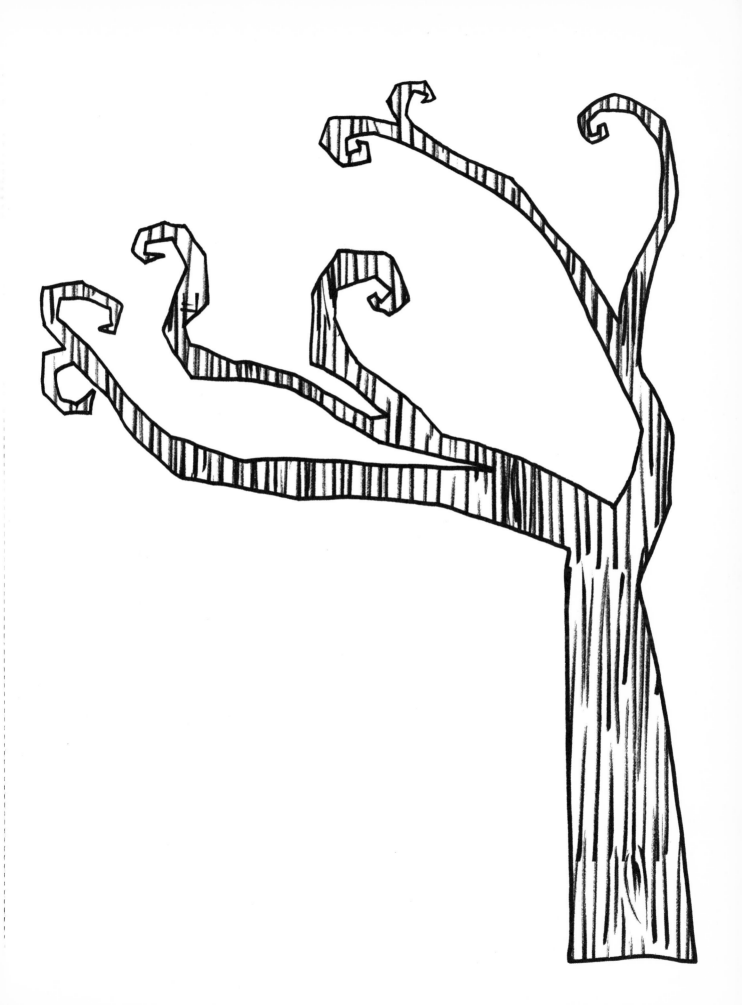

SUMMER SUN

DOODLE LEAVES ON THIS TREE.

PLANTS ON THE MOORS: MOST OF THE PLANTS ON THE MOORS ARE GRASSES, RUSHES, AND HEATHER. HEATHER IS A PRETTY PLANT WITH PURPLE FLOWERS.

FALL INTO FALL

DOODLE AUTUMN LEAVES
ON THE TREE AND GROUND.
WHAT COLOR ARE THEY?

 **HORSES ON THE MOORS:**
IN ENGLAND'S EXMOOR, YOU WILL FIND
THE RARE HORSE BREED THE EXMOOR
PONY. IT IS VERY HARDY AND ADAPTED
TO HARSH CONDITIONS.

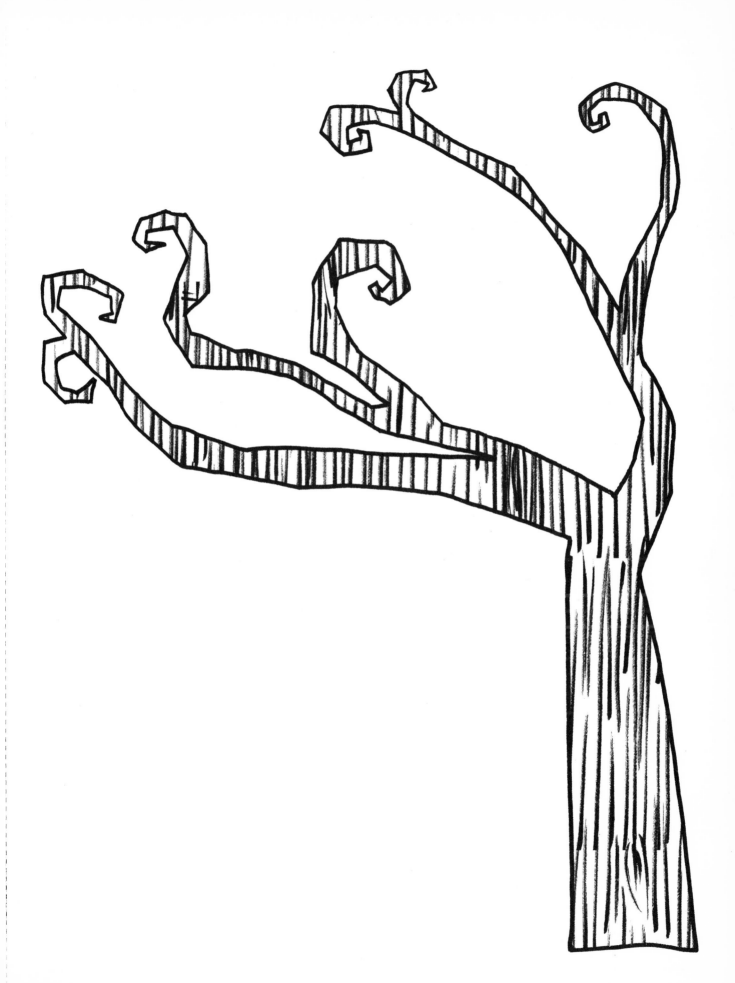

LET IT SNOW!

DOODLE A WINTER SETTING FOR THE TREE.
WILL IT HAVE SNOW ON THE BRANCHES?
WILL IT HAVE ICICLES?
DRAW A SQUIRREL OR A BIRD.

 **SHEEP ON THE MOORS:**
SOME HILL SHEEP BREEDS, LIKE SCOTTISH
BLACKFACE AND LONK, DO WELL ON THE
HEATHER MOORS.

CATHY IS HANGING UP HER LAUNDRY
TO DRY ON THE CLOTHESLINE.
DOODLE IT.

DESIGN DIFFERENT WEATHER VANES ON THE HOUSES ON THE NEXT PAGE. DRAW A ROOSTER, A HORSE, A MERMAID, OR ANYTHING ELSE YOU CAN IMAGINE.

WHO LIVES
IN THE BARN?
⇢⇢⇢⇢

HISTORICAL FOOTNOTE

WEATHER VANE:

A WEATHER VANE IS AN INSTRUMENT PLACED ON THE TOP OF A BUILDING THAT SHOWS WHICH DIRECTION THE WIND IS BLOWING. IT USUALLY HAS LETTERS FOR NORTH, SOUTH, EAST, AND WEST AND AN ARROW OR IMAGE FOR DECORATION.

AN APPLE A DAY

YOU CAN MAKE MANY DELICIOUS
THINGS OUT OF APPLES—
APPLE PIE, APPLESAUCE, AND
CARAMEL APPLES. DOODLE THEM.
WHAT ELSE CAN YOU MAKE?

EGG-CELLENT!

DRAW DIFFERENT DESIGNS ON THESE EGGS.
USE FUN COLORS. TRY DIFFERENT PENS,
MARKERS, CRAYONS, AND GLITTER.

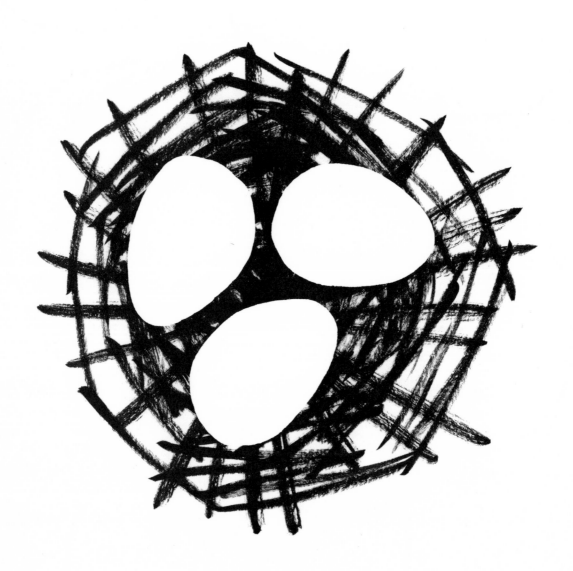

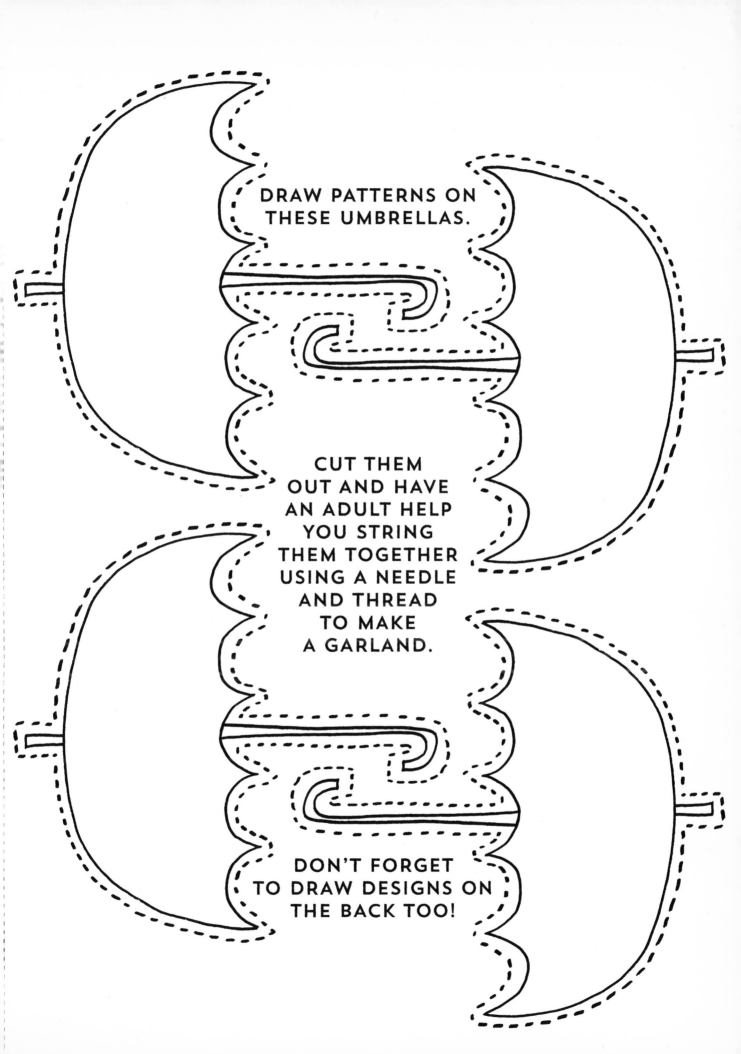

DRAW PATTERNS ON THESE UMBRELLAS.

CUT THEM OUT AND HAVE AN ADULT HELP YOU STRING THEM TOGETHER USING A NEEDLE AND THREAD TO MAKE A GARLAND.

DON'T FORGET TO DRAW DESIGNS ON THE BACK TOO!

DESIGN YOUR OWN SNOWMEN.

Mark Twain

"I HAVE NEVER LET MY SCHOOLING INTERFERE WITH MY DOODLING."

—MARK TWAIN

 AM AN AMERICAN AUTHOR WHO WROTE NOVELS AND HUMOROUS STORIES. BEFORE I BECAME A FAMOUS WRITER, I WORKED AS A MINER, AN APPRENTICE TO A PRINTER, AND A RIVERBOAT PILOT ON THE MISSISSIPPI RIVER. THE WRITER ERNEST HEMINGWAY SAID THAT MY BOOK *THE ADVENTURES OF HUCKLEBERRY FINN* IS THE BASIS FOR ALL MODERN AMERICAN NOVELS.

TWAIN DID FUN DOODLES LIKE THIS ONE...

AND USEFUL DOODLES LIKE THESE TO INDICATE WEATHER CONDITIONS IN HIS BOOK *PUDD'NHEAD WILSON.*

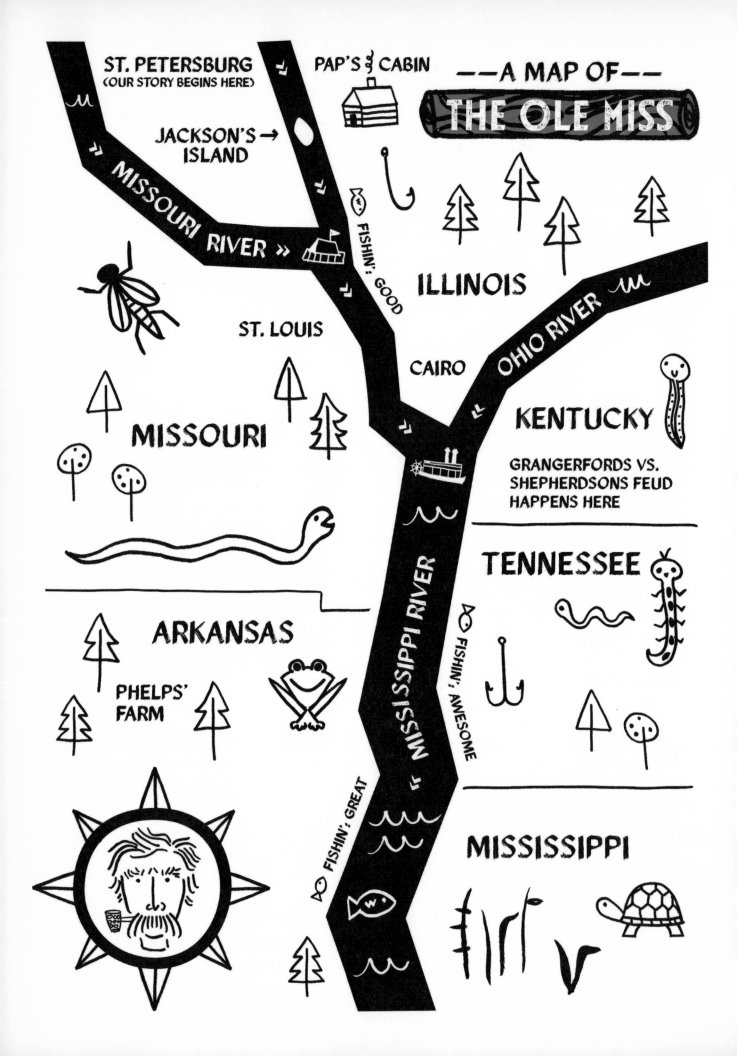

MAP IT

THIS IS THE MAP OF HUCKLEBERRY FINN'S JOURNEY. DRAW A MAP OF SOME PART OF YOUR WORLD. DOES IT INCLUDE YOUR HOME, SCHOOL, FRIEND'S HOUSE, DANCE STUDIO, SOCCER FIELD, OR SOMETHING ELSE?

COLOR YOUR OWN SUNSET.

"EVERYTHING WE HAD IN THE WORLD WAS ON OUR RAFT."

DOODLE ALL YOUR POSSESSIONS.
WOULD THEY ALL FIT ON A RAFT?

PATCH 'EM UP!

JIM'S OVERALLS NEED SOME PATCHES.

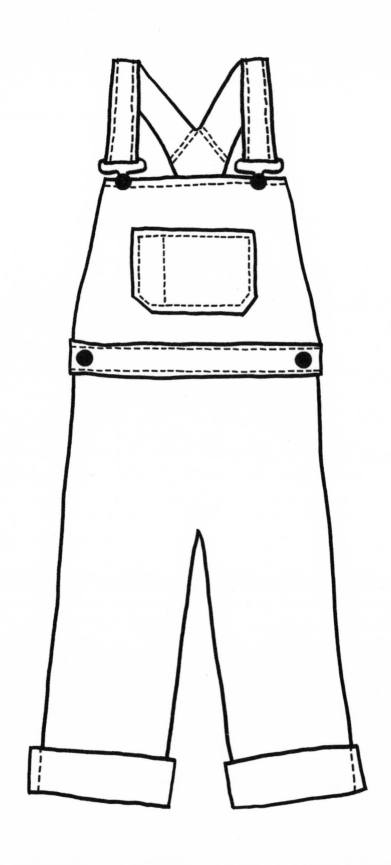

DESIGN OVERALLS FOR YOURSELF.
ARE THEY DENIM? ARE THEY FLOWERED?
DO THEY HAVE PATCHES?

OVERALLS:

THE VERY FIRST BIB OVERALLS WERE CALLED "SLOPS." THEY WERE MADE AS EARLY AS THE 1700s. OVERALLS WERE WORN BY WORKING MEN, SO THEY WERE USUALLY CONSIDERED A SYMBOL OF LOWER-CLASS OR POOR PEOPLE.

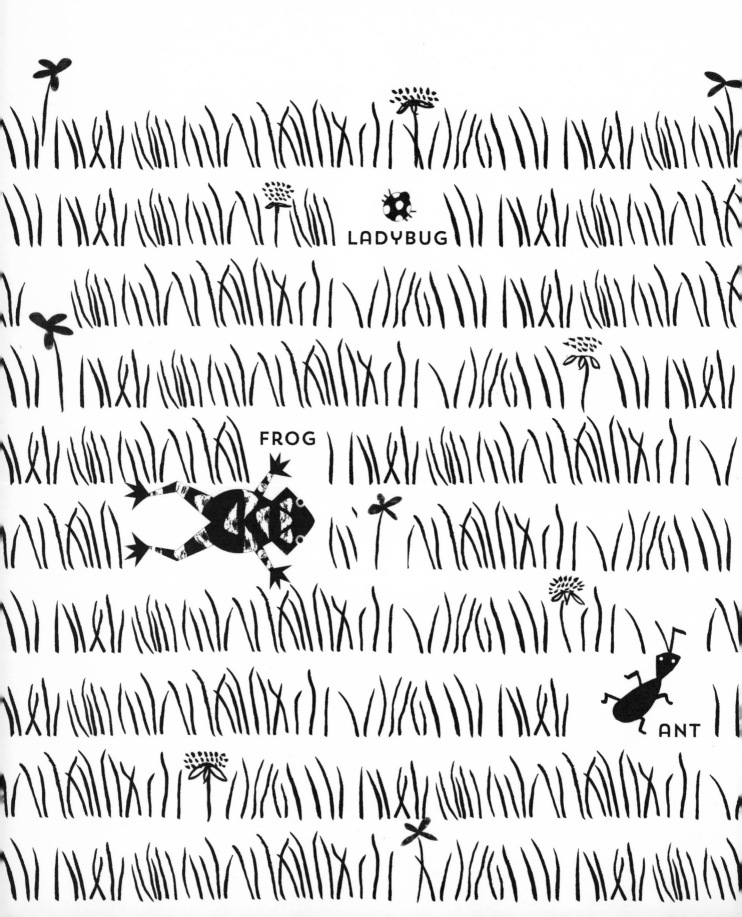

LADYBUG

FROG

ANT

DOODLE MORE INSECTS IN
THE GRASS AND LABEL THEM.

CAN YOU DRAW A CATERPILLAR,
A BEE, AND A DRAGONFLY?
WHAT OTHER INSECTS CAN YOU DRAW?

FRY IT UP IN A PAN

WHAT'S FOR DINNER?

CAMPING TIME

HUCK FINN

HISTORICAL FOOTNOTE

BANDANA:
NEXT TIME YOU GO CAMPING, DON'T FORGET TO BRING A BANDANA. HERE ARE FIVE THINGS YOU CAN USE IT FOR: 1. HAT, 2. WASHCLOTH, 3. WATER FILTER, 4. FLAG, AND 5. SNOT RAG.

DESIGN YOUR OWN BANDANA.

BURNING BRIGHT

FIREFLIES SUDDENLY GLOW IN
THE NIGHT, THEN SEEM HIDDEN AGAIN.
CAN YOU FIND THESE WORDS
HIDDEN IN THE WORD PUZZLE?

FIREFLIES
LANTERN
SPARK
NIGHT
LIGHTNING BUG
LIGHT

STARS
GLOW
SOFT
EVENING
WARM
MAGICAL

HISTORICAL FOOTNOTE

FIREFLIES:
FIREFLIES ARE WINGED BEETLES. THEY
ARE ALSO CALLED LIGHTNING BUGS.
THEY FLASH LIGHT TO COMMUNICATE
WITH EACH OTHER.

```
Y S T N A I R O H P U E G S A
X F E R Q J M D C S L G L O W
B A W I G S F X M K Z D I F J
T D F I R E F L I E S B G T O
A O T A F V L K O H P V H P M
M B T A T E E X J C A E T H K
H S E S C N V M H A R D N D B
T R S E B I C W K D K K I O G
P D Z F B N T D J X E K N C W
Y E C Q C G V R Y L C X G D Q
U D G J W D B N A A Z U B W C
G J K N C F E C E N W L U H N
W E Y C I P I U B T N I G I K
D A Y D V G S J L E N G S S E
X H R J A W H D N R E H S D V
W S E M X J B T M N G T B J U
G J W T U E D V X A I G U E A
```

TRA LA LA

WRITE WORDS FOR THE SONGS
THESE BIRDS ARE SINGING.

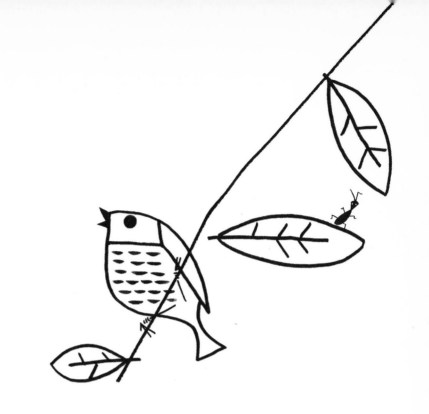

PORTRAIT OF THE ARTIST AS AN OLD MAN

QUOTABLE TWAIN:
MARK TWAIN WAS FAMOUS FOR HIS WITTY SAYINGS AND ONE-LINERS. FOR EXAMPLE, HE CALLED A LITERARY CLASSIC, "A BOOK WHICH PEOPLE PRAISE AND DON'T READ."

DRAW YOUR OWN SELF-PORTRAIT HERE.

"HE DOODLES THE FASTEST WHO DOODLES ALONE."
—RUDYARD KIPLING

I WAS BORN ON DECEMBER 30, 1865, IN BOMBAY, INDIA. I WAS EDUCATED IN ENGLAND AND LIVED IN INDIA, ENGLAND, AND THE UNITED STATES. I AM BEST KNOWN FOR MY SHORT STORIES AND WRITING FOR CHILDREN, INCLUDING *THE JUNGLE BOOK*. I BECAME THE HIGHEST PAID WRITER IN THE WORLD, AND IN 1907 I WON THE NOBEL PRIZE FOR LITERATURE.

KIPLING OFTEN PUT HIS INITIALS IN THE CORNER OF HIS BOOK DRAWINGS, LIKE THIS.

THIS IS FROM "THE ELEPHANT'S CHILD" IN *JUST SO STORIES*.

KIPLING ILLUSTRATED LOTS OF HIS OWN STORIES. THIS IS FROM "THE CAT THAT WALKED BY HIMSELF."

WOLF PACK

MOWGLI WAS PART OF
THE SEEONEE COUNCIL
RUN BY THE WOLVES.
THIS IS THEIR
COUNCIL SEAL.

SEEONEE
COUNCIL

DRAW THE SEAL FOR YOUR FAMILY, CLUB, OR COUNCIL.

NATURE'S PATTERNS

GATHER LEAVES FROM YOUR NEIGHBORHOOD.
SPREAD A LITTLE PAINT ON A PLAIN PIECE OF PAPER.
DAB THE LEAVES IN THE PAINT AND THEN MAKE
PATTERNS ON THIS PAGE USING THE LEAVES.

BALOO

WHAT IS YOUR FAVORITE KIND OF BEAR? IS IT A KOALA BEAR, GRIZZLY BEAR, OR POLAR BEAR?

THESE ARE BLACK BEAR PAW PRINTS

DRAW IT HERE.

EXIT
←≪

ENTER

PEACOCK FEATHERS
ARE BEAUTIFUL!

HISTORICAL FOOTNOTE

FEATHER FACT:
THE PEACOCK IS
THE NATIONAL BIRD
OF INDIA.

PUT A FEATHER ON IT!

DECORATE THESE ITEMS WITH
PEACOCK FEATHER PATTERNS OR COLORS.

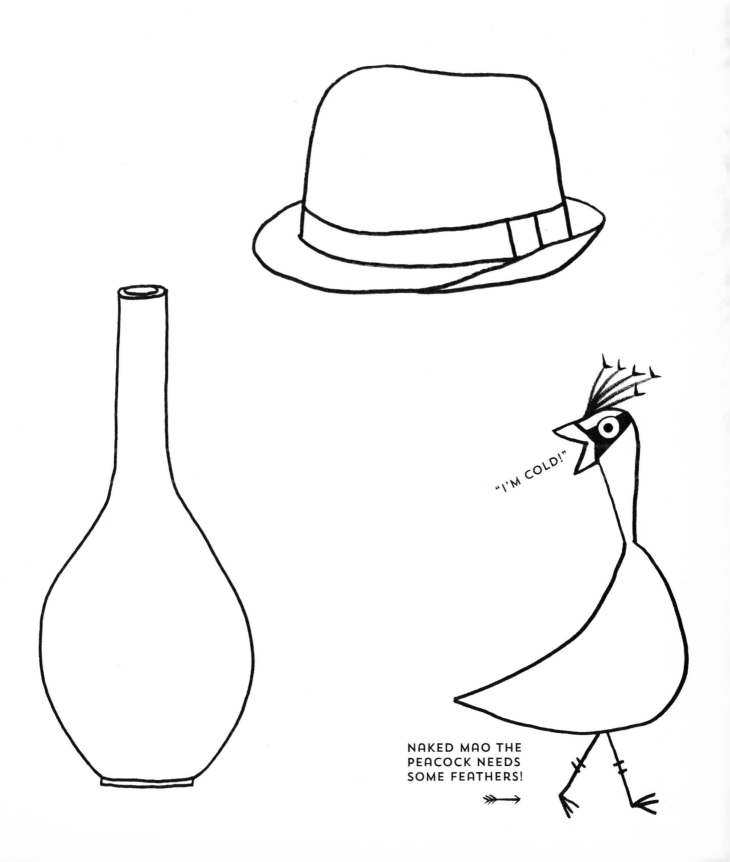

"I'M COLD!"

NAKED MAO THE
PEACOCK NEEDS
SOME FEATHERS!

THIS IS A ZEBRA PRINT PATTERN.
DOODLE THESE OTHER ANIMAL PRINTS.

TIGER

PYTHON

LEOPARD

ATTACK OF THE QUILLS

WHAT CAN YOU DRAW USING THESE PORCUPINE QUILL SHAPES AS A STARTING POINT?

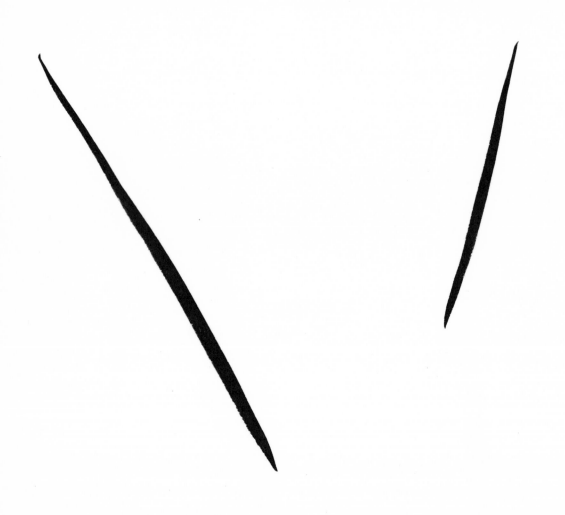

MONKEYS LOVE
BANANAS!

DRAW OTHER FRUIT THAT THE MONKEYS WOULD LIKE TO EAT.

KING OF YOUR JUNGLE

WHAT IS YOUR FAVORITE ANIMAL?
DOODLE IT HERE.

SELF-PORTRAIT OF LEWIS CARROLL ON A WINDY DAY.
MAYBE IT IS THE DAY HE PUBLISHED *ALICE'S ADVENTURES IN WONDERLAND* AND HE IS WORRIED WHAT PEOPLE WILL THINK!

"OH, 'TIS DOODLING, 'TIS DOODLING THAT MAKES THE WORLD GO ROUND."

—LEWIS CARROLL

I WAS BORN IN DARESBURY, CHESHIRE, ENGLAND, ON JANUARY 27, 1832. I ATTENDED SCHOOL AT CHRIST CHURCH, OXFORD, AND THEN TAUGHT MATHEMATICS. ALTHOUGH I WAS SHY, I ENJOYED CREATING STORIES FOR CHILDREN. I'M ALSO THE AUTHOR OF *ALICE'S ADVENTURES IN WONDERLAND* AND *THROUGH THE LOOKING-GLASS*.

SLITHY TOVES

DESIGN THE
SLITHY TOVES.

THE BOROGOVE

THE BOROGOVE IS AN IMAGINARY BIRD.
DRAW OTHER IMAGINARY BIRDS ON THE NEXT PAGE.

 **HISTORICAL FOOTNOTE**

THE BOROGOVE:
THE BOROGOVE IS AN EXTINCT BIRD WHOSE
NATURAL HABITAT WAS THE WABE. THOUGH
FAMED FOR HIS ENORMOUS WINGSPAN, THE
BOROGOVE WAS UNABLE TO FLY.

WHAT DO THEIR FEATHERS LOOK LIKE? HOW ABOUT THEIR BEAKS?

WHAT ARE THE MOME RATHS SAYING?
MAKE UP A SONG OR POEM.
MAKE UP NONSENSE WORDS.

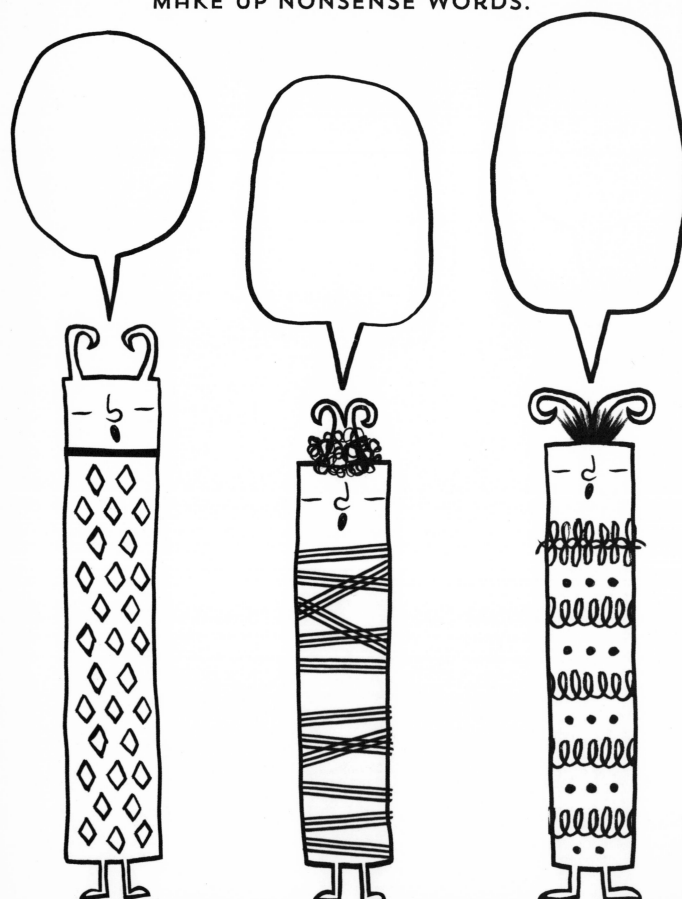

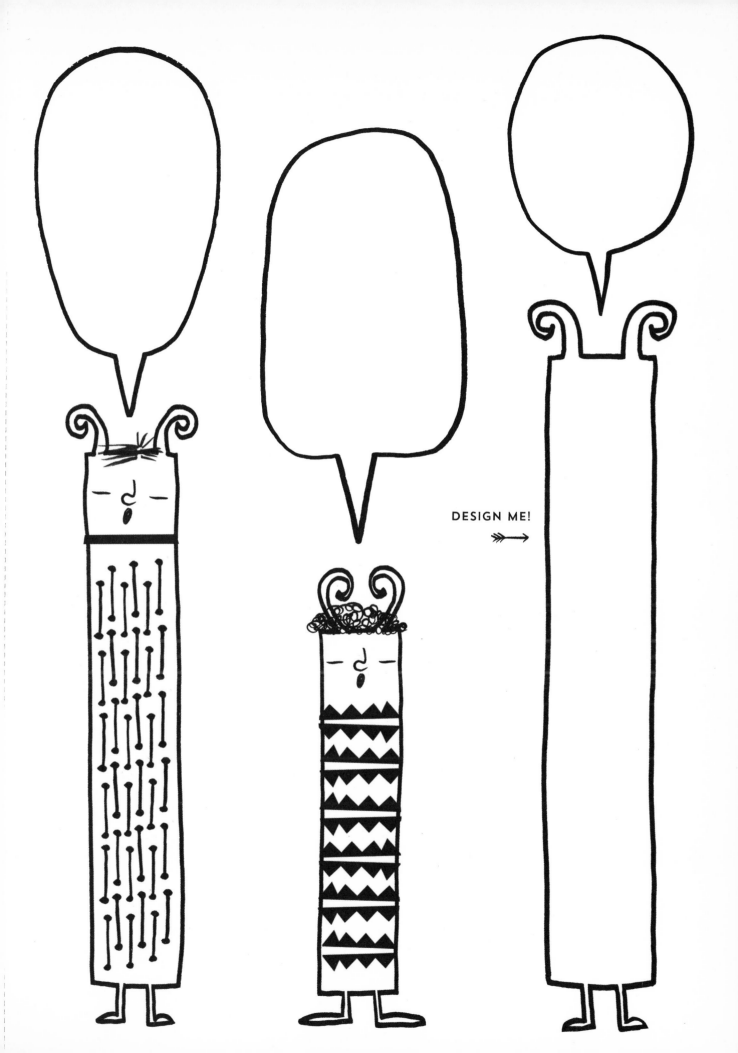

DESIGN ME!
⇒→

FLOWERTARIAN*

DOODLE A PAGE FULL OF FLOWERS
FOR THE JABBERWOCK TO EAT!

* A FLOWERTARIAN ONLY EATS FLOWERS. THE ONLY KNOWN
FLOWERTARIAN SPECIES IS THE JABBERWOCK.

J IS FOR JUBJUB

THE JUBJUB BIRD MAKES THE LETTER "J."
DRAW THE FIRST LETTER OF YOUR NAME,
AND MAKE IT INTO A BIRD.

THE BANDERS

ONE LITTLE BANDER IS PLAYING A TRUMPET
AND ONE IS PLAYING A DRUM.

GIVE THE OTHER BANDERS INSTRUMENTS TO PLAY.

THE TUMTUM TREE

HISTORICAL FOOTNOTE

THE TUMTUM TREE:
THE OLDEST KNOWN TUMTUM TREE IS 25,000 YEARS OLD. IT IS A FAVORITE HIDING SPOT OF THE JUBJUBS AND BLOOMS WITH SPARKLE BERRIES IN BOTH SPRING AND FALL.

DRAW LEAVES, BRANCHES, OR FLOWERS
ON THIS TUMTUM TREE. BE CREATIVE!

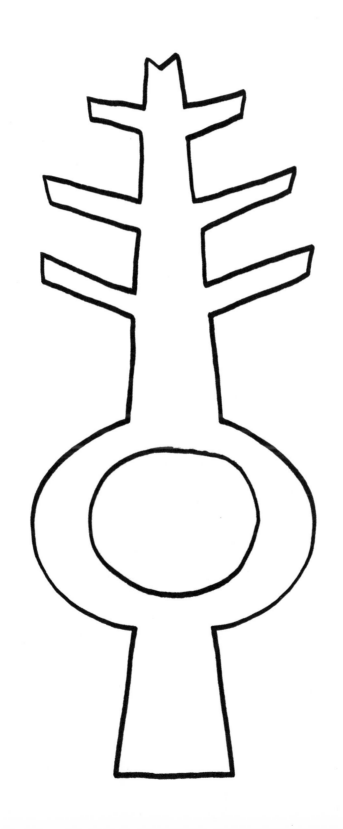

CALLOOH! CALLAY!

MAKE UP OTHER HAPPY WORDS
FOR THESE BANNERS AND COLOR THEM.

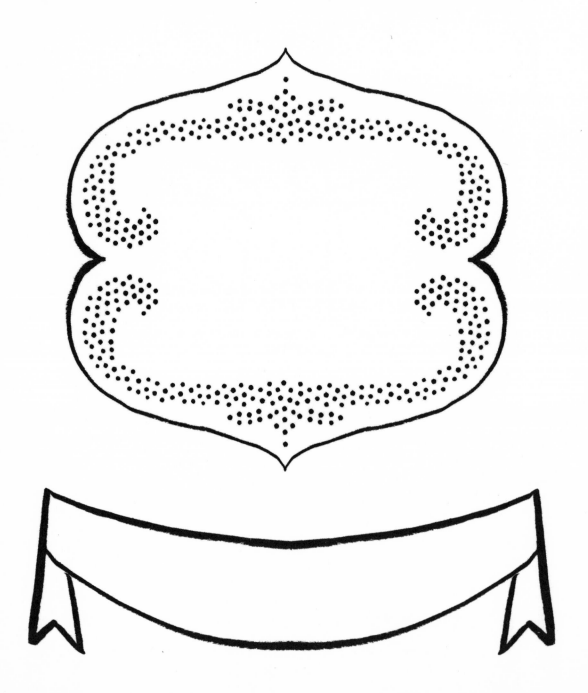

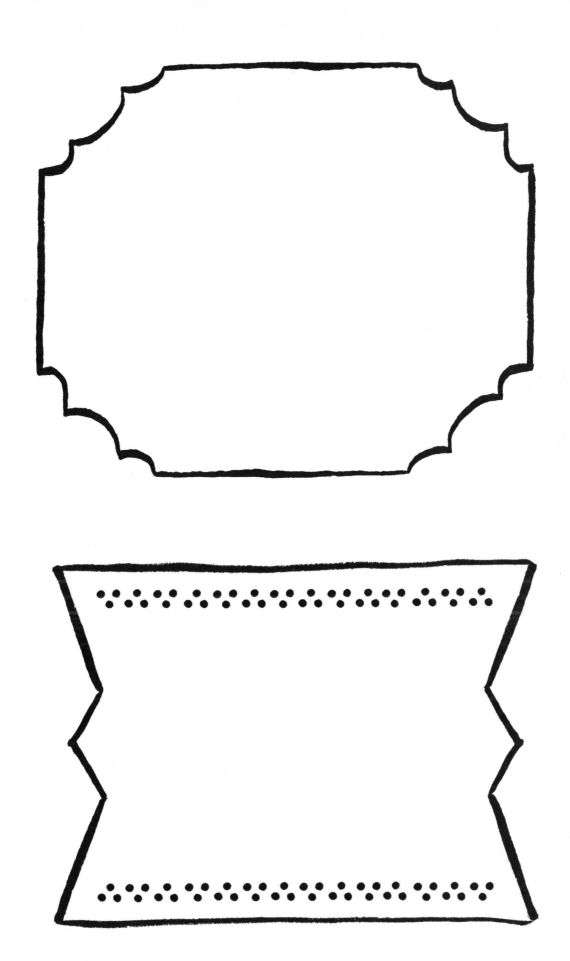

NONSENSE-TIONARY

WHAT DO YOU THINK THESE WORDS MEAN?
GIVE THEM YOUR OWN DEFINITIONS.

BRILLIG: _____

_____

_____

_____

GYRE: _____

_____

_____

_____

GIMBLE: _____

_____

_____

_____

WABE: _____

_____

_____

MIMSY: _____

_____

_____

_____

OUTGRABE: _____

_____

_____

_____

FRUMIOUS: _____

_____

_____

_____

BEAMISH: _____

_____

_____

_____

FRABJOUS: _____

_____

_____

_____

"EVERYTHING THAT I UNDERSTAND, I UNDERSTAND ONLY BECAUSE I DOODLE."

—LEO TOLSTOY

I AM ONE OF THE MOST FAMOUS NOVELISTS OF ALL TIME. I LIVED IN RUSSIA FROM 1828 TO 1910 AND WROTE MANY BOOKS, THE MOST WELL-KNOWN OF WHICH ARE *WAR AND PEACE* AND *ANNA KARENINA*. SOME PEOPLE CONSIDER *WAR AND PEACE* TO BE THE GREATEST NOVEL EVER WRITTEN. I ALSO INFLUENCED RUSSIAN POLITICS LATER IN MY LIFE.

LEO TOLSTOY CREATED MORE THAN 160,000 PAGES OF MANUSCRIPTS! EVEN THOUGH HE DIDN'T THINK HE WAS A GOOD ARTIST, MANY OF HIS MANUSCRIPT PAGES HAD PEN-AND-INK AND PENCIL DRAWINGS LIKE THESE.

AQUARELLE*

USE WATERCOLORS TO FILL
IN THIS BACKGROUND.

*AQUARELLE IS FRENCH FOR "WATERCOLOR." FAMOUS ARTISTS WHO WORKED IN WATERCOLOR INCLUDE WASSILY KANDINSKY, GEORGIA O'KEEFFE, AND PAUL KLEE.

PERFECT PAIRS

DESIGN DIFFERENT EARRINGS.

YOU CAN DESIGN
PAIRS THAT MATCH
OR DON'T

HEEL TO TOE

DESIGN SOME FANCY BOOTS.

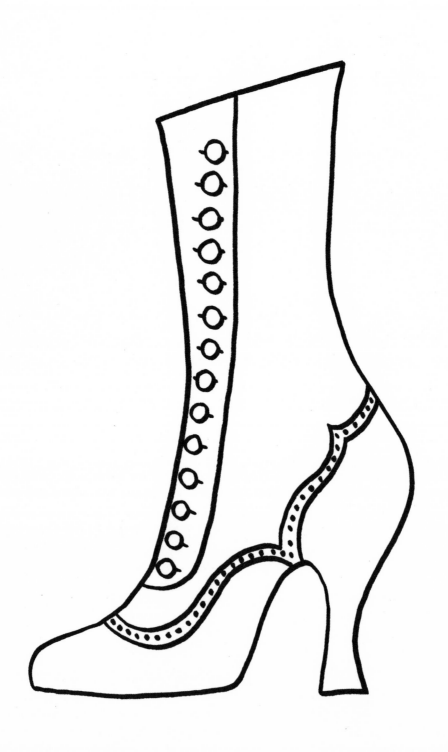

A GOOD HAIR DAY

GIVE ANNA A NEW DO!

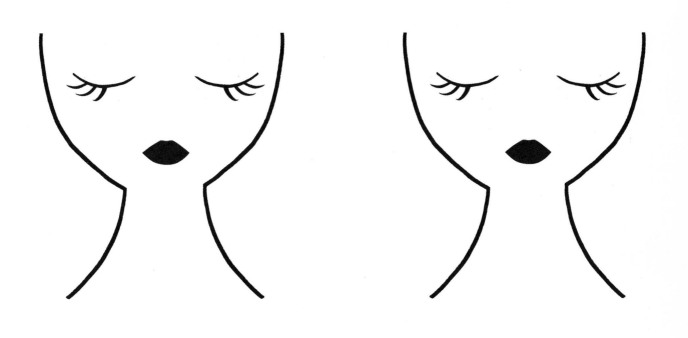

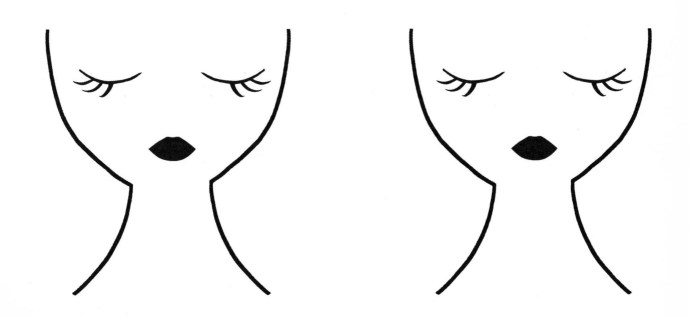

NEED A HAND?

DRAW PATTERNS OR DESIGNS ON THESE GLOVES.
GLUE ON ACTUAL BUTTONS, BEADS, OR LACE.

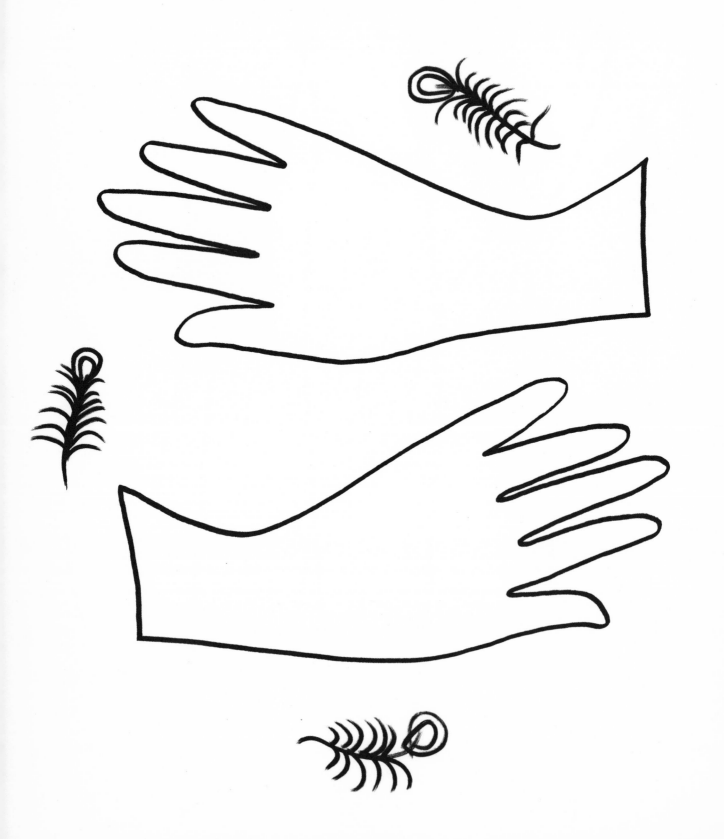

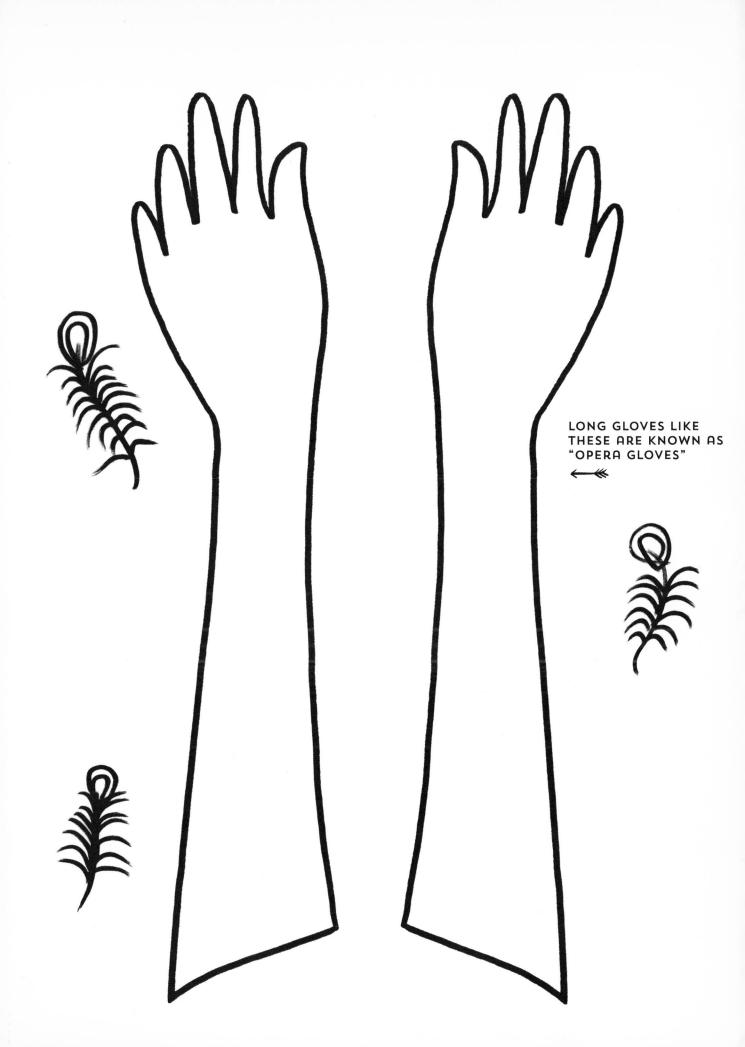

LONG GLOVES LIKE
THESE ARE KNOWN AS
"OPERA GLOVES"
←◄

BE A HANDBAG DESIGNER

ANNA NEEDS A PLACE TO PUT
HER KEYS AND LIPSTICK. DESIGN AN
EVENING BAG FOR HER.

HATS, HATS, HATS!

DRAW A COWBOY HAT, A BOWLER HAT, AND A CHEF'S HAT. WHAT OTHER KINDS OF HATS CAN YOU DRAW?

ANNA'S HAT IS
FOR A DAY AT
THE RACES

FROU-FROU

BUNDLE UP!

DOODLE YOUR OWN WINTER WEAR.
DESIGN GLOVES OR MITTENS, A KNIT CAP,
SNOW BOOTS, A SCARF, AND A WINTER COAT.

FILL THESE VASES
WITH FLOWERS.

CITYSCAPE

ANNA'S IN
MOSCOW

DRAW THE BACKGROUND OF A
DIFFERENT FAMOUS CITY.
IS SHE IN PARIS? LONDON? TOKYO?

JENNIFER ADAMS IS A WRITER AND BOOK EDITOR. SHE IS THE AUTHOR OF MORE THAN TWO DOZEN BOOKS, INCLUDING BOOKS IN THE *BABYLIT®* SERIES, WHICH INTRODUCE CHILDREN TO THE WORLD OF CLASSIC LITERATURE. HER FIRST PICTURE BOOK, *EDGAR GETS READY FOR BED*, IS INSPIRED BY THE CLASSIC POEM "THE RAVEN" BY EDGAR ALLAN POE. JENNIFER LIVES IN SALT LAKE CITY. SHE WORKS ON WEEKENDS AT THE KING'S ENGLISH INDEPENDENT BOOKSTORE. HER FAVORITE CLASSIC NOVEL IS *PRIDE AND PREJUDICE*.

SUGAR IS A DESIGN STUDIO RUN BY DESIGNER AND ILLUSTRATOR ALISON OLIVER. ALISON'S DESIGN PORTFOLIO REFLECTS HER LOVE OF DRAWING, PATTERN, AND COLOR AND INCLUDES EVERYTHING FROM LOGOS TO PACKAGING AND PRODUCT DESIGN. SHE ALSO DESIGNS BOOKS FOR PUBLISHERS INCLUDING CHRONICLE, QUIRK BOOKS, AND GIBBS SMITH, PUBLISHER. SHE IS THE ILLUSTRATOR AND DESIGNER OF THE BOARD BOOKS IN THE *BABYLIT®* SERIES, WHICH INTRODUCE CHILDREN TO THE WORLD OF CLASSIC LITERATURE. ALISON LIVES IN NEW YORK CITY. HER FAVORITE CLASSIC NOVEL IS *ALICE IN WONDERLAND*.